FRESH AIR AFFAIRS

Written with
Kathryn O'Shea-Evans

Principal photography by
Tara Sgroi

RIZZOLI
NEW YORK

New York · Paris · London · Milan

Lela Rose

FRESH AIR AFFAIRS

ENTERTAINING WITH STYLE IN THE GREAT OUTDOORS

To my parents, Rusty and Deedie Rose, who always loved a good outdoor party.
And to my own alfresco family: Brandon, Grey, and Rosey, who always RSVP yes.
(And help me cook, set the table, do dishes, and everything in between.)

Contents

Introduction

Anyone who has ever attended my fashion shows knows that they're anything but standard-issue. Actually, they're not fashion shows at all. They're a *party*. And because one of my favorite things to do is host events outdoors, where there's enchantment in every puffy cloud and flitting bird, I hold most of my shows alfresco. (The flattering natural light is just a bonus.) When you're invited to a Lela Rose show, you might *think* you're headed to a sleek warehouse, but you're more likely to end up on a pier overlooking the glimmering Hudson River, watching models strut down a runway of yellow rose petals. Or find yourself in Washington Square Park, where—instead of sashaying—our models played chess, read the *Financial Times*, and tossed birdseed to felt pigeons before some very real interlopers joined in.

When you're outdoors, you and your guests are practically guaranteed to experience a little unexpected magic. That's why when I knew I wanted to write my second book on entertaining, I also knew it would be about hosting dreamy (yet doable!) events *outside*. It's similar to that time-honored concept of dinner and a show. When you host under the open sky, you provide the dinner, and nature provides the show . . . whether that's a jaw-dropper of a pink sunset at your cocktail hour (see page 228), or cows mooing cacophonously in a neighboring field as you serve up a Texas cheese plate (see page 38). In the freshness of outdoor air, you can count on unexpected thrills both large (impromptu snow in April!) and small (like a rainbow-hued painted bunting landing briefly in a bush right as you look, as if to say "Hey, y'all.")

I decided to organize this book into four sections that cover all of my favorite areas to host alfresco: at our Texas ranch ("On the Range"); among the twinkling lights of Manhattan and Dallas ("Civil Ceremony"); in rolling pastureland ("Farther Afield"); and along the river and in the thick forests of our mountain home in Jackson Hole, Wyoming ("Mountain

Majesty"). But just because these parties happened in the places I love doesn't mean you can't do them in yours—each one can be tweaked and tailored to your own locale, using your own regional ingredients and tipples. Party-worthy outdoor event spaces can be found anywhere, from Orlando to Omaha! What matters is being together in the fresh air, and enjoying life's not-so-guilty pleasures.

One of my "musts" when hosting events is finding inspiration for the food, decor, wardrobe, and more in my surroundings. It's something that I did for each and every event you'll see in this book. Entertaining full throttle like this is such an obsession of mine that I installed everything from a table that comes down from the ceiling at the push of a button to a tequila bar in my Tribeca home. As you might have guessed, I love to transform spaces and things! And no outdoor space is off-limits.

Years ago I was hosting a secret fashion show in Tribeca, and I asked all of our top editors and buyers to show up at a neighborhood park. As they waited, sipping Topo Chico proffered by handsome waiters and probably wondering what on earth was happening, I stood around the corner with eighteen models (all dressed and ready to go) *and* a marching band

of twenty musicians . . . and then we felt giant raindrops—the ones that suggest a monsoon-like New York City downpour is imminent. Now, trombones and tubas can't get wet, and models in full hair and makeup don't take too kindly to it either. I thought, Oh . . . this may be the one outdoor event that I regret. We're in trouble! But we decided the show must go on. And as the band started playing Beyoncé's "Crazy in Love," we marched uproariously down the street, New Orleans-style. All of a sudden, the clouds opened up above us and rays of sunshine beamed down like a spotlight on our merry parade. We were making a ton of noise, and random people started joining us, popping out of restaurants and offices. A little boy even tugged his mom down from their apartment into the throng, telling her: "Mom, do you hear the music? We have to go down and dance!"

See what I mean about hosting events outside? It was spellbinding, and it never, ever would have happened if we had kept to ourselves in some bland indoor space, confined within a box. Even if it had rained, a little drizzle would have been worth it just for the memory. That's what this book is about: stepping out into the world with your favorite people and celebrating life together in unforgettable style.

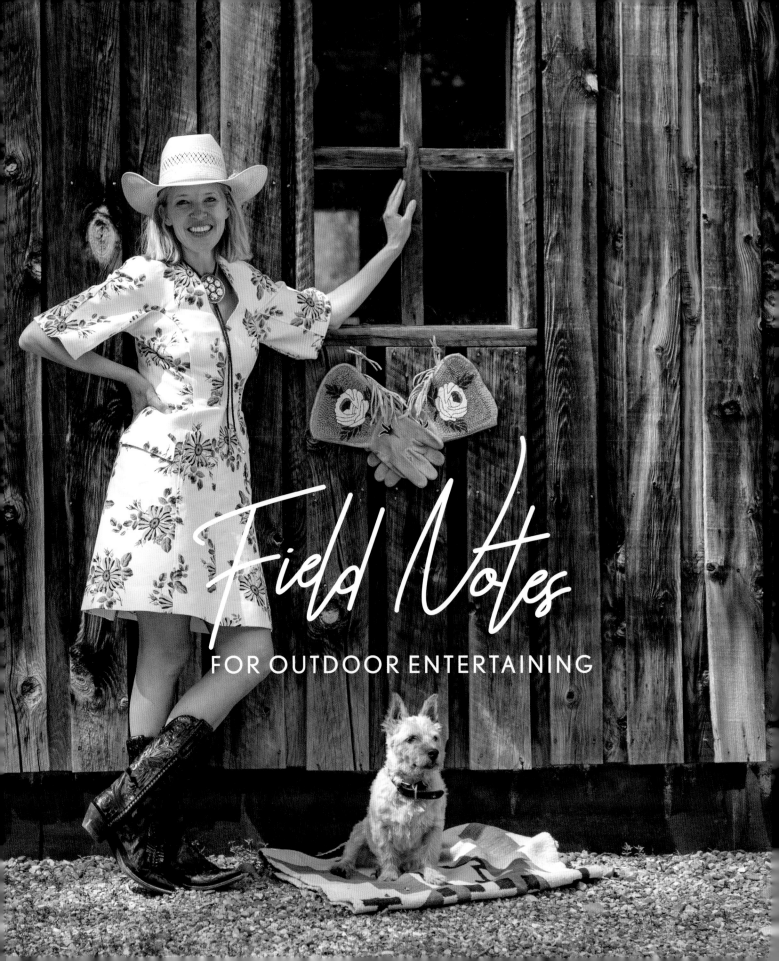

Field Notes

FOR OUTDOOR ENTERTAINING

Because I host so many events outside, where anything can happen, people are always asking me what my Plan B is. I tell them that my Plan B is for Plan A to work! Still, there are a few sanity-saving measures you can take to ensure your guests—and, just as importantly, *you*—have a fabulous time.

Get Your *You-Know-What* Together

Smaller fetes can be planned last-minute, like the cactus cocktail hour on page 32, which I dreamed up mere hours in advance. But for larger events, I always begin corralling ideas on my Pinterest boards at least six to eight weeks ahead. It's not because I think parties are all that much better when every little decision is mulled and agonized over. It's because one of my greatest joys in hosting is coming up with details, so I savor this time. Embroidering napkins with stars to suit a celestial theme, shopping Etsy into the wee hours for the perfect place cards . . . why cut all of that excitement short?! As the saying goes, the devil is in the details—and I take that to mean the host will have a devilish time coming up with them.

When it comes to the food, I am not a "wing it" kind of girl. That's a recipe for disaster. Even though I have cooked my entire life and pretty much know what I'm doing, if I haven't tried a particular recipe before, it doesn't go on the party menu. Can you imagine how nightmarish it would be to make something new for twenty people? So don't do it. Try recipes well in advance for your family, who are practically required by law not to complain too much when your prime rib is subprime, or your flounder, well, flounders.

Preparation Makes Perfect

Nobody likes a stressed-out host. The best way to achieve a happy, easygoing vibe is to prep, and prep early. That way, by the time the event rolls around, you're ready to kick up your own heels, too. Did you know that your salad dressing can be made three days ahead? And that even a soufflé can be mixed a day ahead of time and plopped in the refrigerator ready to bake? Figure out what you can do in advance (like setting the table the night before) and then actually do it, so you take as much as possible off your plate for the day of the event. Believe me, you don't want to be frazzled and fried when your guests show up . . . and they don't want that either.

Find Your Muse

No, you don't need to add billows of smoke to a cocktail to make guests feel special (although if you want to try it, see page 110). But whenever you're getting your friends together, go the extra mile. That doesn't mean spending a lot more money—it just means using your creativity to think of a few tiny details that they'll always remember. Take the linens at the lunar-inspired event on page 100: instead of the standard black or white, I used napkins with a celestial print. If you're getting the itch to host but don't have a muse in mind, look to your favorite surroundings. When I'm in Texas at our ranch and I know that the gorgeous fields of bluebonnets and Indian paintbrush are blooming, I think . . . OMG, I want to go sit in that field and be in those flowers, it's so stunning! And yes—a party quickly ensues.

Have *Fun*

I love to start a party right by showing guests some TLC: I always greet them with a smile and a signature cocktail, which makes a huge difference. It lets them know immediately that they're going to have a great time. It's one of the easiest ways to demonstrate that you've thought of a special detail just for them, and it's so much more welcoming and charming than saying, "The bar is over there—go make your own drink!"

Let Go

Grab yourself a glass of water (and by water, I mean tequila), head to your medicine cabinet, and take a big chill pill . . . because with any event, things can and *will* go wrong. Expect it. It's just part of the fun, and it's what makes parties memorable.

On the Range

There's a reason artists like Donald Judd flocked to Texas. There's little more inspiring than the billowing clouds over our prairies and the transcendent light that glows down from our wide-open skies. When I'm in my home state, I can't help but gasp, "How gorgeous is this?!" and think of ways to toast Texas in all its glory.

Off the Wagon

A VERY ON-BRAND COCKTAIL HOUR

ike most people, I went a bit stir-crazy during the Covid-19 quarantine. So I decided to create cocktails for Instagram next to an old barn wagon at our Texas ranch . . . and my "off the wagon" cocktail series was born. I just couldn't help myself. The wagons of Wild West fame are right there, awaiting their cheeky close-up! And nothing juxtaposes more beautifully with well-worn wood than shocking pinks. Because I'm constantly espousing the importance of matching your drink and your dress to your table—in color or in tone—I really went for it during this cocktail hour, serving blush-pink blood orange margs that I call rosaritas. Even the elevated tostadas —topped with watermelon radishes and dragon fruit—were pink, their tortillas transformed with beet juice into a deep magenta hue. Talk about tickled pink!

ROSE-COLORED TOSTADAS WITH WATERMELON RADISH AND AVOCADO CRÈME
Makes 12

These color-rich tostadas combine a luscious avocado crème with tender chicken, spicy jalapeño and radishes, and lightly sweet dragon fruit. The pink tortillas, colored with red beets, are dramatically delicious, but the tostadas are equally tasty when made with fresh corn tortillas.

12 small (5-inch diameter) pink tortillas, warmed (see note)
Avocado-Lime Crème (recipe follows)
8 ounces shredded poached chicken
1 medium watermelon radish, quartered and very thinly sliced
1 small dragon fruit, trimmed and diced
1 large jalapeño, stemmed, seeded, and finely diced

AVOCADO-LIME CRÈME
Makes about 2½ cups

2 large avocados, pitted, peeled, and sliced
1 cup coarsely chopped fresh cilantro
1 cup pepitas (green pumpkin seeds), toasted
½ cup fresh lime juice
⅓ cup extra-virgin olive oil
2 jalapeños, stemmed and seeded
2 garlic cloves, peeled
1 teaspoon fine sea salt

Combine all the ingredients in a blender and blend until smooth. (The crème can be prepared up to 1 day ahead. Cover and refrigerate.)

BLOOD ORANGE ROSARITA
Makes 8 to 12

A "rosarita" is my signature blood orange margarita. If you can't find blood oranges, you can substitute orange juice.

3 cups silver tequila
2 cups fresh blood orange juice
1½ cups Cointreau or other orange-flavored liqueur
½ cup fresh lime juice
¼ cup blood orange syrup, such as Monin
Chili-lime seasoning, such as Tajín
Lime wedges
Ice cubes
Dried blood orange slices for garnish (optional)

Stir the tequila, blood orange juice, Cointreau, lime juice, and syrup to blend in a large pitcher. Fill a small plate with a thin layer of the chili-lime seasoning. Run lime wedges around the rims of cocktail glasses to moisten. Press the rims into the salt to coat. Fill glasses with ice. Divide the margarita among the glasses. Garnish with dried blood orange slices, if desired, and serve.

¼ cup fresh cilantro leaves
Salt
Lime wedges

Spread the warm tortillas with Avocado-Lime Crème and arrange on a very large platter. Top the crème with some of the chicken, radish, dragon fruit, jalapeño, and cilantro. Sprinkle lightly with salt and serve with fresh lime wedges.

Note: Pink tortillas can be sourced or you can make your own by using beet juice in place of water in your favorite corn tortilla recipe or packaged mix.

PREVIOUS PAGES: I fancified the tortillas by turning them pink with beet juice. THESE PAGES: Freshly squeezed juice is the key to a top-notch marg. I rimmed the glasses with Tajín Clásico Seasoning (a mix of chili, lime, and sea salt).

Flights of Fancy

A BIRD-WATCHING BOONDOGGLE

y father was a serious birder—I would even say he was a semiprofessional ornithologist. He knew everything about every bird you would see, from a white cattle egret to a cobalt blue indigo bunting—including its foraging habits and flight patterns. That's no small feat in the state of Texas, with its 600-plus species!

Because Texas is key to North America's bird populations—one in every three migrating birds in the US soars through the state—it's a celebratory place to experience the spring and autumn migrations. But you don't have to live in Texas to flock with your own friends on a bird-watching safari.

I used our bird-watching adventure as an excuse for, *ahem, cockatiel* hour. We set out pre-sunset, when the air was cooling off, with some tipples that would make my dad proud: a pisco sour, the lemon peel skewered with found feathers (sanitized, of course). I served them in old stainless steel cups I'd bought in India—they are lightweight and unbreakable, and they keep your drink ice-cold. Engine off, it wasn't long before we were stretched out on the woven early American coverlet in the truck, western meadowlarks and vermilion fly-catchers filling the skies around us.

OPPOSITE: Safaris are truly great, but have you ever been bird-watching in Texas? April is prime time, thanks to the spring migration. LEFT: Turkey feathers and vines I've found walking through the fields of our ranchland in Texas. PREVIOUS PAGES: Carved wooden birds—including a woodpecker, sandpiper, and quail—my grandmother collected for my dad from an artist in East Texas.

PISCO SOUR WITH RHUBARB AND HONEY SYRUP
Makes 2

¾ cup pisco brandy
1 egg white
¼ cup fresh lemon or lime juice
¼ cup Rhubarb and Honey Syrup (recipe follows)
Ice cubes
Angostura bitters
Lemon zest curls for garnish (optional)

Mix the pisco, egg white, lemon juice, and syrup in a cocktail shaker. Add ice and shake vigorously (or I prefer a blender) until the mixture is frothy. Pour into chilled cups or glasses, dividing evenly. Top the drinks with a dash or two of bitters and garnish as desired.

RHUBARB AND HONEY SYRUP
Makes about 2 cups

2 stalks rhubarb, cut into ½-inch pieces
1 cup water
½ cup honey
½ cup sugar

Combine the rhubarb, water, honey, and sugar in a medium, heavy saucepan. Bring the mixture to a boil over medium heat. Reduce the heat to low and continue to simmer until the rhubarb is very soft, about 6 minutes. Cool. Strain the syrup into a jar and discard the solids. (Syrup can be made 2 weeks ahead. Keep refrigerated.)

Anything bird-related is so inspirational and fun. LEFT: I'm wearing our Lela Rose Birds of a Feather pinafore dress with a vintage roadrunner belt. OPPOSITE: Sanitized feathers adorn a pisco sour made with rhubarb-honey syrup and egg white froth—clearly, I love to stay on theme!

LEFT: Cardinals and cedar waxwings adorn the boots, which I designed and had handmade for me by a fabulous boot maker, Rex Klingelhefer, in Mason, Texas. (He's old-school—he doesn't have a phone but will tell you to come back on a certain date and they'll be ready.) ABOVE AND OPPOSITE: I paired vintage quail plates my mom found at an estate sale with unbreakable metal tumblers I picked up in India years ago. Among my geometric tablecloths of choice for outdoor events? A hand-loomed, timeworn nineteenth-century American coverlet.

JALAPEÑO PEPPER JELLY RELISH

Makes about 2½ cups

Serve this chunky spicy-sweet relish with grilled poultry, such as the quail nibs (see Resources) wrapped in bacon pictured here.

1 (12-ounce) jar pickled jalapeño slices,
   drained but juices reserved, chopped
3 tablespoons sugar
1 tablespoon coriander seeds, toasted and coarsely ground
2 small apples, peeled, cored, and finely diced
1 (4-ounce) jar diced pimentos
3 large jalapeño peppers, stemmed, seeded, and diced
Salt
Black pepper

Combine the pickled jalapeño juices with the sugar and coriander seeds in a medium, heavy saucepan. Add the apples and simmer over medium heat until the apples are tender and the liquid is reduced to a thick syrup, about 10 minutes. Stir in the chopped pickled jalapeños and simmer 1 minute for the flavors to meld. Transfer the relish to a bowl and stir in the pimentos. (Can be prepared up to 3 days ahead. Cover and refrigerate.)

Just before serving, mix in the fresh jalapeños and season to taste with salt and coarsely ground pepper.

THIS PAGE AND OPPOSITE: On a birding day I love to serve grilled bacon-wrapped quail nibs I order from Texas Quail Farms, a sustainable company in Lockhart, Texas. They're absolutely delicious, especially paired with jalapeño pepper jelly relish.

Prickly Please

CACTUS COCKTAIL HOUR

ne recent weekend afternoon at our ranch just outside Dallas, I made prickly pear margaritas inspired by the cactus dotting the surrounding landscape. Prickly pear cactus is famous for its candy-red fruit, often used to make agua fresca in Mexico. It tastes a bit like melon and it added sweetness to the margs, but I was even more excited about its transfixing ruby color.

To bring everything together, I used fresh cactus cuttings in the flower arrangements and studded the tomatillo salsa with edible cactus, too. That's something you could do with other types of produce, like jicama, as well. I just love an unexpected element in a recipe . . . it makes guests think, Ooh, *funnn*. And isn't that the point?

CACTUS AND POBLANO SALSA
Makes about 3 cups

3 poblano peppers
1 tablespoon olive oil
1 pound well-cleaned nopales (cactus paddles),
   diced (about 3 cups)
Salt
¾ cup purchased or homemade salsa verde,
   from one (7-ounce) can
½ cup diced red onion
1 red jalapeño or Fresno chili, stemmed, seeded,
   and finely diced
2 tablespoons finely chopped cilantro

Char the poblanos over a gas flame or under a broiler until blackened and charred on all sides. Transfer to a bowl and cover with plastic, allowing the poblanos to steam while cooling. Peel, seed, stem, and dice the poblanos.

Heat the oil in a 10-inch cast-iron skillet over high heat. Add the nopales, sprinkle with some salt, and stir briefly. Reduce the heat to medium, cover, and cook until the nopales have released their jellylike juices, about 10 minutes. Stir once and continue to cook, covered, until the juices have evaporated and the nopales just begin to brown, about 10 minutes. Stir in the poblanos and salsa verde and simmer until slightly thickened, about 3 minutes. Transfer the salsa to a bowl and cool. Mix in the onion, red jalapeño, and cilantro. Serve with chips.

PRICKLY PEAR PUNCH
Makes 6

1 cup mezcal
1 cup silver tequila
¾ cup Prickly Pear Syrup (recipe follows)
¼ cup fresh lime juice
1 lime
Flaky sea salt
1½ cups lime-flavored seltzer, chilled

Stir the mezcal, tequila, syrup, and lime juice to blend in a pitcher. Refrigerate until well chilled.

Finely grate the lime zest and cut the lime in half. Fill a small plate with flaky sea salt. Add the lime zest and stir to combine. Run the cut lime around the rim of six glasses to moisten; dip the rims into the salt mixture. Stir the seltzer into the pitcher, divide among glasses, and serve.

OPPOSITE: For this cactus-themed cocktail hour, I served Prickly Pear Punch in a set of fabulous Italian cocktail glasses etched with saguaro cacti and rimmed with salt and lime zest. I am often every bit as laser-focused on how something looks as how it tastes, because let's be honest: the first sense that we engage with is visual! ABOVE: A cactus-and-poblano salsa.

PRICKLY PEAR SYRUP
Makes about 2 cups

6 pink prickly pears (tunas)
1½ cups water
1 cup sugar
¼ cup fresh lime juice

Using a large, sharp knife and wearing gloves or using tongs to hold the fruit, cut the prickly pears in half. Carefully spoon the pink flesh and seeds from the fruit into a heavy saucepan. Add the water and sugar and stir over medium heat until the sugar dissolves and the mixture boils. Reduce heat to low and simmer until the prickly pear is very tender and the mixture thickens slightly, about 20 minutes. Cool completely. Transfer the mixture to a blender and pulse briefly to puree. Strain the syrup into a jar, discard the solids, and stir in the lime juice. (Syrup can be made 2 weeks ahead. Keep refrigerated.)

Dairy Queens

AN ONLY-IN-TEXAS CHEESE PLATE

would not call myself a bona fide cowgirl, but I love a good longhorn. And when it comes to Texas exports, our cheeses should rank nearly as high as our oil and propane—and legendary Willie Nelson. They're great, and they could have cheesemonger destinations like France and Italy quaking in their barn boots. So during a recent cattle drive on the ranch, I thought . . . Why not celebrate it the best way I know how with a "Bigger and Better" Texas Cheese Board? No matter where you live, you can consult your nearest cheesemonger and create a cheese plate of regional deliciousness.

Any local cheesemonger will tell you there are a few absolute musts, including raw milk goudas and aged cheddars. One of my favorite Texas cheeses is robiola incavolata, which was invented in Piedmont, Italy; here it is nestled in cabbage leaves for extra cream factor. (And it's actually a goat cheese . . . don't tell the cows!) Given our locale, I served them all on a timeworn wood table I found in our barn with plenty of crisp cracker options and a teetering tower of jalapeño slices. Hey, it's Texas. Don't mess with it.

I love nothing more than enjoying a blissful spring afternoon at the ranch: billowing clouds, bright blue skies, and some darling heifers. They are very curious creatures and are headed toward me as if to ask, "Hey, girl! Can you mooove over?"

BOURBON BROWN COW FLOAT

Makes 4

1 pint vanilla ice cream
1½ cups chilled horchata
1 cup ice cubes
¾ cup bourbon
Ground cinnamon
Cinnamon sticks

Combine the ice cream, horchata, ice, and bourbon in a blender. Blend until smooth. Divide the drink among glasses. Sprinkle the drinks with cinnamon, garnish with the cinnamon sticks, and serve.

OPPOSITE: To honor our unbelievable ranch hands (except the kids, of course!), I served up a frothy take on a velvet hammer in vintage sundae glasses with rose gold straws. (For the uniniti-ated, it earned that moniker because it goes down smooth like velvet but hits you hard like a hammer in the morning!)

BIGGER AND BETTER
TEXAS CHEESE BOARD

A locally sourced cheese board is great fun wherever you live. Ask your favorite cheesemonger for suggestions—and don't forget local fruit or honey!

Clockwise from bottom left:
Candied Jalapeño Chevre (Haute Goat Creamery)
Van Sormon (Brazos Valley Cheese)
Moultonzola (Lira Rossa)
Fat Tailed Tomme (Veldhuizen Cheese)
Robiola (Lira Rossa)
Araguaney (Dos Lunas Cheese)
Buttercup (Haute Goat Creamery)

The secret to a luxurious local cheese plate is keeping it simple: consult your nearest gourmet cheesemonger on the best options in your area, then add a regional honey and a couple of nut and cracker options. I served this one on a thick slab of wood I found in our barn with wrought iron serving pieces.

Haymaker

ELEVATING THE BARNYARD BARBECUE

Hay is for way, way more than horses. Whether you're throwing a barn wedding or a garden party in the countryside, you can transform the flaxen dried grass into an utter indulgence. For this recent barbecue I held in and around our old barn, we gave hay bales a bit of an interior design treatment with custom tufted seat cushions in ginghams galore. We even used hay as an ethereal garnish for a bourbon cocktail called the Spiced Ginger Haymaker. Humble, ever-satisfying cowpoke food got upgrades, too: We wrapped baked beans in a cast-iron pot swirled with bacon to cook over the fire and elevated Texas toast by branding brioche bread slices with a cast-iron lasso-style brand I ordered on Etsy.

Because I hosted the main dinner inside the barn itself, I couldn't help but emphasize the romance factor. We set our table with a palette of Texas sky blues and earth browns; flanked it with supple leather director's chairs; and lined the walls around it with bales of sweet-scented hay. The only issue with all that straw? We couldn't light candles. But between the glowing guests and peals of twinkling laughter, we didn't mind.

PREVIOUS PAGES: We constructed a room within a room in our barn out of hay bales—and it smelled amazing. OPPOSITE: Blooming artichokes dotting the tablescape have all the architectural prettiness of purple alliums. The 1950s enamelware plates are edged in the cattle-brand alphabet.

SPICED GINGER HAYMAKER
Makes 2

Sugar
1 orange, zested
1 lime, zest finely grated and lime halved
Ice cubes
¼ cup bourbon
¼ cup fresh orange juice
2 tablespoons fresh lime juice
1 tablespoon Cointreau
1 tablespoon ginger simple syrup

Fill a small plate with a thin layer of sugar, and stir in the orange and lime zests. Run the cut lime up the side of two old-fashioned glasses to moisten and dip the glasses into the sugar to coat. Fill the glasses and a cocktail shaker with ice. Add the bourbon, orange juice, lime juice, Cointreau, and syrup; shake well. Strain the cocktail into the glasses and serve.

THESE PAGES: We edged the rims of our Spiced Ginger Haymaker cocktails with a little citrus pixie dust and a hay knot. Being a little "extra" is *so* worth it at parties!

THESE PAGES: It's easy enough to have custom cushions made that will totally steal the show; just enlist your seamstress or trot out your trusty old Singer sewing machine. With contrasting tufting and ruffled edges, these gingham numbers are as sweet as a Texas pecan pie—a fun touch that lends so much style to the scene. They are tailor-made for cozying up on the humble hay bale!

BRANDED TEXAS TOAST WITH SHALLOT-THYME BUTTER
Makes 12 servings

At the ranch we like to "grill" our Texas toast with our brand (see Resources).

1 cup (2 sticks) butter, at room temperature
1 shallot, minced
1 teaspoon minced fresh thyme leaves
1 garlic clove, minced (optional)
12 thick slices brioche or sandwich bread, from 1 loaf

Preheat a grill to medium. Stir the butter, shallot, thyme, and garlic, if using, in a small bowl until well blended. Spread a thick layer of the butter on the bread slices. Grill the bread until toasted and lightly browned, then turn and brown the other side, about 2 minutes total. Serve warm.

To brand the toast: Heat a brand over hot coals until very hot. Gently press the brand into the toast until browned.

Fancify your Texas toast with brioche bread (served here with shallot-thyme butter) and a personalized brand. I had this one made by an artisan on Etsy to look like a lasso-style brand, with an *R* for Rey Rosa—our ranch. Just heat it up in the fire and let it make its mark.

BACON-WRAPPED CHILI BEANS

Makes 12 servings

I serve the beans with slow-cooked shredded pork and creamy coleslaw.

1 pound black beans	½ teaspoon ground allspice
1 pound pinto beans	¼ teaspoon ground cinnamon
¼ cup bacon drippings or vegetable oil	¼ teaspoon ground cloves
3 medium onions, chopped	12 ounces dark Mexican beer
1 head garlic, cloves finely chopped	3 cups water
1 (3-ounce) package ancho chili powder, about ⅔ cup	2 teaspoons dried Mexican oregano
2 tablespoons ground cumin	3 tablespoons masa harina
	2 teaspoons kosher salt
	2 to 3 pounds sliced bacon

Combine the beans in a very large bowl. Add cold water to cover the beans by 3 to 4 inches and soak overnight.

Drain the beans and set aside. Heat the bacon drippings in a very large Dutch oven over medium-high heat. Add the onions and sauté over medium heat until golden brown and tender, about 10 minutes. Stir in the garlic and cook for 2 minutes. Add the ancho chili, cumin, allspice, cinnamon, and cloves and stir until fragrant, about 1 minute. Add the beer and stir, scraping up the browned bits from the bottom of the pan. Mix in the water, beans, and oregano. Simmer over low heat, stirring occasionally, until the beans are just tender, about 1 hour.

Sprinkle the beans with the masa harina and salt. Simmer, stirring occasionally, until thickened to chili consistency and the beans are very tender, about 45 minutes longer. Cool, cover, and refrigerate. (Can be prepared up to 3 days ahead.)

Arrange bacon slices, overlapping slightly and extending halfway over the edge of a cowboy cauldron or hanging Dutch

THESE PAGES: Baked beans are nobody's idea of elegant party food. But yes, even *they* can be upgraded! These were beautifully wrapped with bacon—almost like a present—within a cast-iron pot, then hung over the flickering fire until ready to serve.

oven until the edge is lined with bacon completely. Spoon the beans into the cauldron and smooth the top. Fold the bacon slices over the top of the beans, enclosing the beans completely. Hang the pot over a medium-hot fire and cook until the beans are heated through, about 1 hour. Meanwhile, heat the cauldron or Dutch oven lid directly in the coals of the fire until very hot, about 45 minutes. Carefully remove the cauldron or Dutch oven from the fire. Using tongs, carefully place the heated lid atop the cauldron or Dutch oven and allow to stand until the bacon is lightly browned and the lid cools to warm, about 20 minutes. Serve the beans with pieces of bacon.

Pecan Pride

EASY NIBBLES THAT NEVER FAIL

F un fact: The pecan is the state tree of Texas. It's also the only tree nut that is indigenous to North America, its name taken from the Algonquin word for "nuts requiring a stone to crack." I've been nutty about the tree's sweet, buttery seeds since childhood, when we'd venture into my grandmother's yard and pick fallen pecans right off the ground. At least, the ones the squirrels hadn't gotten to yet!

This recipe, Grandsue's Sweet and Spicy Roasted Pecans, is one of my favorite recipes in the book and a total ode to my childhood days picking pecans. They're the perfect umami-rich blend of spicy, sugary, salty, and sweet, thanks to the cumin, chili pepper, brown sugar, honey, and butter galore. (Listen, people, I never said they were healthy.) They're a great thing to make ahead of a party, and you can also keep them in your hosting arsenal for when friends drop by unannounced—or set them out on your counter to snack on at any time. For this afternoon cocktail hour, I served the nuts alongside toasted pecan old-fashioneds in iridescent glasses. The nuts themselves last up to a month, I'm told, but I've never actually tested that . . . in my house they always disappear in a matter of days.

Pecans were a formative snack during my Texas childhood; we grew up cracking them open to fish out the meat with fun accoutrements, like these vintage nut crackers that belonged to my grandmother. In adulthood I'm just as addicted, and these spicy yet sweet nuts are my absolute favorite recipe for them.

GRANDSUE'S SWEET AND SPICY ROASTED PECANS

Makes about 6 cups

6 tablespoons (¾ stick) unsalted butter
3 tablespoons dark brown sugar
3 tablespoons honey
2 teaspoons ground cinnamon
1½ teaspoons cayenne pepper
1½ teaspoons salt
1 teaspoon freshly ground black pepper
1 teaspoon chili powder
¾ teaspoon ground cloves
½ teaspoon ground ginger
6 cups pecan halves
Fresh rosemary for garnish

Preheat the oven to 325°F. Line two large, heavy sheet pans with silicone liners or parchment paper. Melt the butter in a large, heavy saucepan over medium heat. Add the brown sugar, honey, cinnamon, cayenne, salt, pepper, chili powder, cloves, and ginger and stir briefly. Cook the mixture, without stirring, until the brown sugar dissolves and the syrup bubbles. Remove from the heat. Add the pecans and stir gently with a silicone spatula until they are evenly coated with the syrup. Spread the pecans out in a single layer on the prepared sheet pans. Cook the pecans in the oven until they just brown, about 15 minutes. (Do not burn.) Cool pecans completely on the sheet pans on rack. (Pecans can be prepared up to 1 week ahead. Transfer the pecans to jars or to an airtight container and keep in a cool, dry place.) When ready to serve, garnish with rosemary.

OPPOSITE: You can roast and serve Grandsue's Sweet and Spicy Roasted Pecans in the same dish! I prefer a low, wide one that's easy for guests to access, which helps ensure that there won't be any fisticuffs over them. (Yes, they're that good!)

PECAN OLD-FASHIONED
Makes 1

Pecan-flavored cocktail syrup, such as Proof, is a combination of toasty pecans, bitters, and aromatics. You can add more bitters to taste.

Sugar
Finely grated orange zest (reserve 1 strip of peel)
Ice cubes
¼ cup Belfour Texas Pecan Wood Bourbon or other pecan bourbon
2 tablespoons pecan cocktail syrup, such as Proof
Angostura bitters, optional
Fresh rosemary sprig for garnish

Fill a small plate with a thin layer of sugar and stir in the orange zest. Fill a cocktail shaker and an old-fashioned glass with ice. Add the bourbon and syrup to the shaker. Add a dash or two of bitters if desired and shake well. Strain the drink into the glass, garnish with a strip of orange peel and a rosemary sprig, and serve.

OPPOSITE: Pecan Old-Fashioneds are better than plain ole old-fashioneds by a mile, especially with a sprig of rosemary and an orange zest rim.

Raise One for Rusty

(A Drink for Dad)

A SIPPABLE SONNET

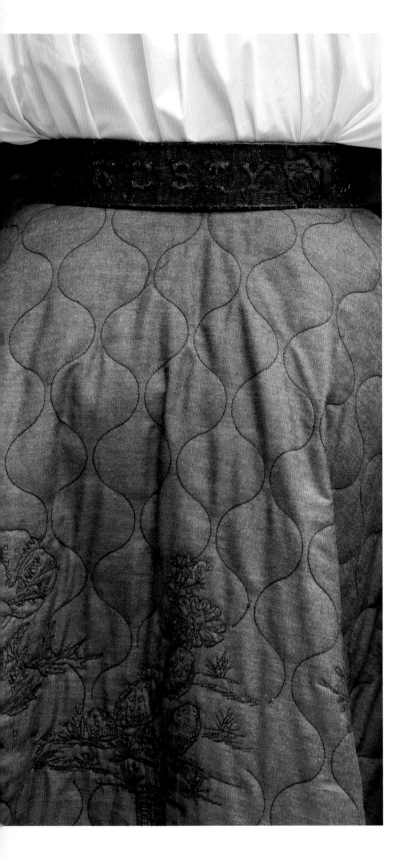

My dad's name was Rusty Rose. He sounds a little like a larger-than-life character from a John Wayne movie, doesn't he? But that's what he was: cinematic. A wonderful, fabulous man who inspired me in so many ways my entire life. He didn't drink Rusty Nails—the cocktails invented in New York in 1937 and made from scotch and Drambuie, a herbaceous whiskey from Scotland—but I still serve them every once in a while as a nod to him. And I make them with my dad's old silver barware, which was made by the amazing Tucson silversmith Frank Patania in the 1930s. I collect a lot of Navajo and American Indian vintage sterling pieces and love Patania's creations; I'm forever on the hunt for his work.

To kick these Rusty Nails up a notch, I added roasted peach and a garnish of Texas blossoms (not edible, but certainly pretty!) in each glass. We served the drinks with a panzanella salad—a tangy Tuscan classic with stale crusty bread and tomatoes—reborn with a decidedly Texas twist thanks to cornbread and roasted peaches. The peaches are another ode to my dad, who adored them. Cheers to you, Rusty!

PREVIOUS PAGES: The belt buckle I'm wearing over my quilted Rey Rosa denim skirt was crafted by famed Tucson silversmith Frank Patania. LEFT: My dad hand-tooled this belt at summer camp when he was twelve years old. OPPOSITE: My dad's jiggers and other barware, also made by Patania.

ROASTED PEACH RUSTY NAIL
Makes 4

1 ripe peach
1½ cups blended Scotch whiskey
4 tablespoons Drambuie
Ice cubes
Peach slices for garnish
Sage and lavender sprigs for garnish

Preheat the broiler to high. Line a small, heavy pan with foil. Cut the peach in half and arrange, pit included, cut side up on the prepared pan. Broil the peach until well browned. Cool completely. Place the peach halves in a jar along with any juices in the pan. Cover the peach with the whiskey and steep to flavor the whiskey for 2 to 6 hours. Discard the peach.

Fill a cocktail shaker and four glasses with ice. Add the infused whiskey and Drambuie to the cocktail shaker. Shake well. Strain the drink into the glasses, garnish with peach slices and sage and lavender sprigs, and serve.

OPPOSITE: Fresh lavender and sage for garnish.
RIGHT: Served up in an asymmetrical vodka glass, a Rusty Nail cocktail becomes all the more alluring with the addition of roasted peaches for sweetness.

GRILLED CORNBREAD AND PEACH PANZANELLA
Makes 6 to 8 servings

1 (8-inch-square) pan of cornbread, cut into 1-inch cubes
1 cup extra-virgin olive oil, divided
1/3 cup red wine vinegar
1 tablespoon honey
2 garlic cloves, crushed
1 scant teaspoon salt
2 teaspoons fresh thyme leaves
6 peaches, pitted and sliced
4 cups cherry tomatoes, halved
1 hothouse cucumber, quartered lengthwise and sliced
1 small red onion, sliced
1/2 cup torn fresh basil leaves, plus more for garnish
8 ounces burrata cheese, cut into pieces

Preheat the oven to 375°F. Toss the cornbread cubes with
1/4 cup of the olive oil on a sheet pan. Toast the bread in the oven
until golden brown, about 10 minutes.

Whisk the remaining 3/4 cup olive oil, vinegar, honey, garlic, salt,
and thyme in a large bowl. Add the toasted cornbread,
peaches, tomatoes, cucumber, onion, and basil to the bowl
and toss gently to combine. Top the salad with the burrata and
more basil leaves and serve.

LEFT: Infuse your olive oil with fresh thyme to increase the
flavor. OPPOSITE: Fresh burrata and top-notch olive oil . . .
swoon! This salad is an "only in Texas" take on the classic Italian
panzanella, with grilled cornbread, cucumbers, peaches,
basil, and . . . of course . . . burrata for days.

Civil Ceremony

Entertaining comes naturally in the big city, where there are often more cocktails per capita than in any rural hamlet. But when you have Michelin-starred restaurants down the block, you've got to get creative to wow friends new and old. My secret is to do what few restaurateurs can: host alfresco.

Raze the Roof

PUMP IT UP

Occasionally, the more unexpected your event locale is, the better the event. One of my all-time favorite places to entertain is a defunct pump house next to my parents' home in Highland Park, Texas, that they restored for that very reason. Yep, a pump house. Surrounded by industrial cement walls (replete with exposed rebar!) with nothing above you but lush trees and starry skies and a thin layer of glass-like water underfoot, you feel like you're part of an art installation at MoMA.

For my latest, I leaned in hard to the fantasy of it all—bringing in elements of *Alice in Wonderland*; Antoine de Saint-Exupéry's 1943 novella *The Little Prince*, with its lone rose; and Brit fashion photographer Tim Walker. As dusk fell, we projected the image of a floating rose onto a concrete wall. On the evening's menu were edible roses suspended in diaphanous gelatin; flower-laden salads to satisfy any Mad Hatter; and ice cubes for each wineglass that were cut like diamonds and filled with a single rose. By the end of the night, the guests were black-tie and barefoot, and soon we were dancing—kicking up water like kids after a summer rain.

PREVIOUS PAGES: Stepping into the pump house is like passing through a portal into another world. OPPOSITE: Never a dull detail! These chairs were designed by Warren McArthur in the 1940s for conference rooms in New York City's Chrysler Building—complete with hidden ashtrays under the armrests.

LILLET SPRITZ WITH ROSE CRYSTAL ICE CUBES
Makes 8

Ice cubes
1½ cups citrus-flavored vodka
¾ cup torn fresh basil leaves
1 (750 ml) bottle Lillet Blanc, well chilled
Floral ice cubes (see Resources) or other ice cubes
About 8 ounces tonic water to finish (optional)

Fill a cocktail shaker with ice. Add the vodka and basil to the shaker and shake vigorously. Strain the vodka into a small pitcher and divide among 8 wineglasses. Top the vodka with the Lillet, dividing it evenly. Add ice cubes to the glasses and top with tonic water, if desired.

PREVIOUS PAGES: On our reflective plexiglass tabletop, I mingled my grandmother's old cut-crystal glassware with glasses I picked up on holiday in Italy. "Jewels" of ice that we ordered from Los Angeles–based Disco Cubes give this simple Lillet Spritz an eye-candy element.

THESE PAGES: A handful of candlesticks straight out of *Alice in Wonderland* add to the wondrous scene. Set at varying heights, they create a skyline for the eye to wander, delighting high and low. FOLLOWING PAGES: An elegant molded dessert continues the midcentury vibe. I used double-sided tape under these floral frogs so that they could securely hold rose stems upright and not tip over.

CHAMPAGNE-ROSE VINAIGRETTE
Makes about 2 cups

½ cup extra-virgin olive oil
½ cup grapeseed oil
½ cup Champagne vinegar
¼ cup honey
¼ cup minced shallot, about ½ large shallot
2 tablespoons fresh lemon juice
1 teaspoon salt
½ teaspoon rose water

Whisk the ingredients in a bowl. Transfer to a jar and seal. (Vinaigrette can be prepared up to 2 days ahead and refrigerated. Allow vinaigrette to come to room temperature before using.)

PREVIOUS PAGE AND LEFT: My grandmother's cut crystal has been "raising a glass" for generations. OPPOSITE: An apple a day keeps the doctor away, but a flower salad a day will keep you on cloud nine—especially when it's served with a rose water vinaigrette. FOLLOWING PAGES: The drippier the pink and red taper candles in them, the better! PAGES 90-91: We projected a single floating rose onto the Pump House's concrete walls after dusk.

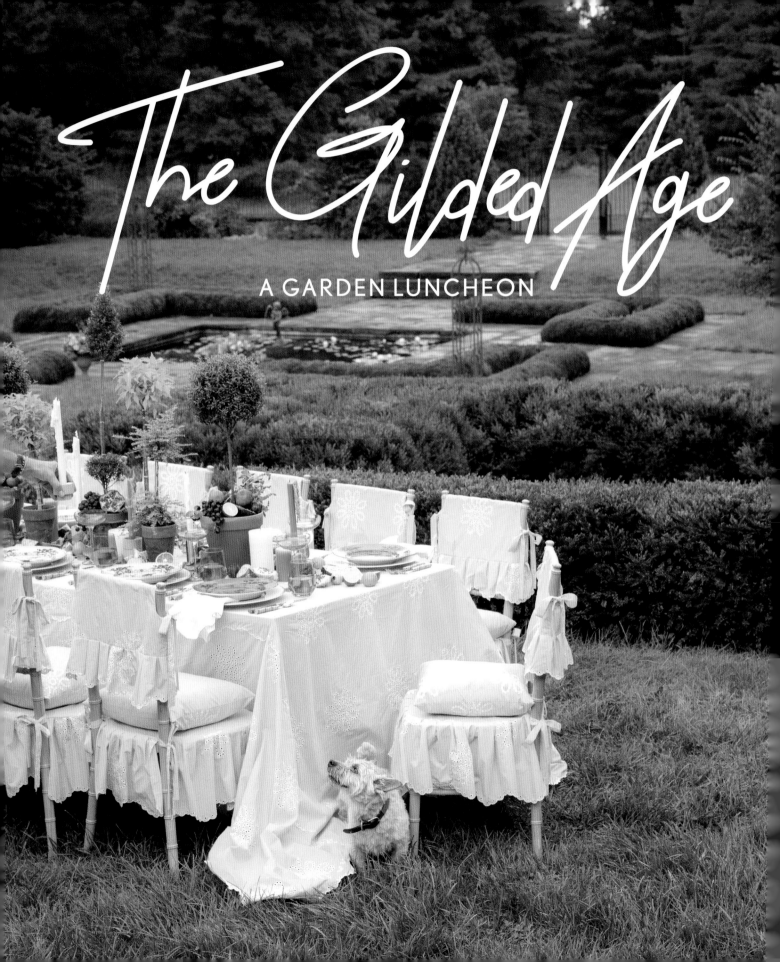

The Gilded Age

A GARDEN LUNCHEON

I should moonlight as a location scout, because I'm forever searching for captivating party locations in and around New York City. When I stumbled across the grounds of this 1842 Greek Revival manse, I nearly pinched myself. In a city of hidden gems, the Bartow-Pell Mansion—with its manicured gardens complete with gurgling fountains and ornate hedges—is the jewel in the crown.

I knew instantly that it would be a fabulous place to throw a Wharton-worthy garden luncheon of tea sandwiches and Gilded Age gimlets, with candy-hued gowns required. To zhuzh things up a bit, we enlisted one of our in-house seamstresses to hand-make covers for the table and chairs from citrine broderie anglaise fabric. (We even made pillows so guests felt comfortable lingering a while!)

On the tabletop, topiaries of every type echoed the manicured grounds. Over and around them, we copiously overflowed fresh fruits—whole and cut (rubbed with a bit of citrus to preserve them). It looked like a Dutch still life in real life. I do love flowers, but grapes, cut pomegranate, and dragon fruit are the most textural, gorgeous things, and unlike hydrangea, they won't wilt in the heat.

What better place for a sumptuous garden luncheon than the lush grounds of a nineteenth-century Gilded Age estate? Look for storied home tours in your area; you'll likely find one that is willing to be a cinematic backdrop for your own garden party for a fee.

GILDED AGE GIMLET WITH POMEGRANATE
Makes 1

Ice cubes
¼ cup vodka
2 tablespoons pomegranate juice
1 tablespoon fresh lime juice
1 tablespoon simple syrup
Holy basil sprig for garnish (optional)

Fill a cocktail shaker with ice. Add the vodka, juices, and simple syrup and shake vigorously. Strain into a coupe glass and garnish with holy basil, if desired.

THESE PAGES: Gilded Age Gimlets with Pomegranate and gem-colored dinnerware have the same power to transfix as glittering nineteenth-century diamond and ruby brooches, lending timeless glamour to the table.

UPPER CRUST TARTINES
Makes 24

12 slices Pullman-style sourdough or firm white bread,
    crusts removed
12 to 16 ounces softened goat cheese, cream cheese,
    or mascarpone
1 pint mixed cherry tomatoes, halved
2 tablespoons extra-virgin olive oil
2 teaspoons minced fresh oregano
12 ripe figs, stemmed and quartered
Holy basil, basil, or mint leaves
2 Persian cucumbers, peeled lengthwise into thin ribbons
2 green onions, sliced very thinly
2 red jalapeños, stemmed, seeded, and sliced very thinly
Flaky sea salt
Freshly ground black pepper

Toast the bread slices until golden. Cool, then halve the slices
diagonally, making 24 toasts. Spread the toasts with a thin
layer of cheese and arrange on serving plates. Toss together
the tomatoes, olive oil, and oregano in a small bowl. Spoon
the tomatoes onto 8 toasts. Arrange the figs and basil leaves
atop another 8 toasts. Layer the cucumber, green onion, and
jalapeño slices atop the remaining 8 toasts. Sprinkle the
tartines with sea salt and pepper, and serve.

THESE PAGES: For those of you who were thinking, Fig-gedabou-
tit!, yes, figs really do grow in New York City.
To make these summery tartines, we topped artisanal toast
slices with goat cheese and figs or tomatoes or cucumber.

Moon over Manhattan

ROOFTOP REVELRY

One of my main goals with any party is to dress up and drink. (*Clink, clink.*) Truman Capote must have had the same hankering when he threw his infamous Black and White Ball at the Plaza Hotel in 1966. He invited so many luminaries—Andy Warhol! Gloria Vanderbilt! Audrey Hepburn!—that New Yorkers experienced FOMO for decades afterward.

Capote's color palette that night was black, white, and chic all over, which served as my inspiration for this Moon over Manhattan dinner party. I held it at dusk on my friend's Fifth Avenue rooftop, where a cinematic span of skyscrapers twinkled around us.

As any Broadway set designer will tell you, the beauty is in the details. To set a palpably glamorous tone, I ordered a mirrored piece of acrylic to sit on the tabletop and reflect the surrounding skyline. I sewed constellations onto my black napkins, adding sequins and rhinestones for a bit of shimmer.

As my guests headed home, I treated them to one final touch: a favor bag containing breakfast in bed for the next morning, including a baguette, moon-shaped butter dusted with black sea salt, and charcoal water—a rumored hangover cure. Capote would have loved it.

THESE AND FOLLOWING PAGES: I found inexpensive models of iconic Manhattan skyscrapers—like the Empire State and Flatiron Buildings—on Etsy, then spray-painted them all the same glitzy silver hue. Slim taper candles of varying heights echoed the cityscape in a warm and welcoming shade of cream, each nestled in a Ted Muehling Egg & Dart candlestick.

OPPOSITE: I chose the marbleized chargers underneath the plates since they looked like full moons. THIS PAGE: I've always adored the art deco lines of the Chrysler Building, which opened in 1930, and used its era signage to inspire the place cards.

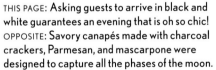

THIS PAGE: Asking guests to arrive in black and white guarantees an evening that is oh so chic! OPPOSITE: Savory canapés made with charcoal crackers, Parmesan, and mascarpone were designed to capture all the phases of the moon.

MISTY MOON OVER MANHATTAN
Makes 1

On special occasions I hire a bartender to help with the drinks.
The Red Moon is a red wine variation of the classic Manhattan
cocktail, and I added the bump of cherry flavor. My bartender
created the over-the-top presentation, complete with cherry-
wood smoke and gold-leaf-covered Amarena cherries (gold leaf
is available to order online), but I assure you, it's equally delicious
without the wisps of smoke and precious metal.

Ice cubes
¼ cup dry red wine
2 tablespoons bourbon
1 scant tablespoon cherry syrup
Dash of Angostura bitters
Sphere-shaped ice or other large ice cube
Orange peel for garnish
Sprig of fresh thyme for garnish
Amarena or other cocktail cherries for garnish

Fill a cocktail shaker with ice. Add the wine, bourbon, syrup, and
bitters and shake vigorously. Place the ice sphere into a glass.
Strain the cocktail over the ice. Garnish with the orange peel,
thyme sprig, and cherries.

THESE PAGES: For my signature cocktail that night,
I served Misty Moon over Manhattans, each
adorned with edible gold-leaf-gilt cherries and smoke.
Guests were nothing less than starry-eyed!

ÎLE FLOTTANTE

Makes 6 servings

Île flottante is a classic French dessert in which eggs and cream are conjured into a rich custard sauce surrounding an island of soft meringue. The desserts can be garnished with caramelized sugar sprinkles or spun sugar, if desired.

SAUCE
1 cup whipping cream
½ cup whole milk
4 whole eggs, separated, plus 2 yolks
⅓ cup sugar
1 teaspoon vanilla extract

ISLANDS
butter, for greasing
⅔ cup sugar, plus more for coating
4 egg whites (½ cup)
Pinch of salt

FOR THE SAUCE: Bring the cream and milk to a simmer in a medium, heavy saucepan. Whisk the egg yolks and sugar in a medium bowl until light. Gradually whisk the hot cream mixture into the yolks. Return the yolk mixture to the saucepan and stir over medium-low heat until the mixture thickens to coat the back of a spoon, about 3 minutes. (Do not boil.) Remove from the heat and pour into a bowl. Stir in the vanilla. Cool completely and chill. (Can be prepared up to 2 days ahead, covered and refrigerated.)

FOR THE ISLANDS: Preheat the oven to 350°F. Generously butter 6 ½-cup soufflé cups. Lightly coat the soufflé cups with sugar. Using an electric mixer, beat the egg whites with a pinch of salt in a large bowl until soft peaks form. Gradually beat in the ⅔ cup sugar and continue beating until stiff and glossy. Divide the egg whites among the prepared soufflé cups, mounding slightly in the center. Bake until the egg whites puff and are beginning to lightly brown, and a tester inserted near the center comes out clean, about 12 to 15 minutes. Cool to room temperature, at least 20 minutes and up to 3 hours. (The meringues will deflate as they cool.)

Divide the custard sauce among 6 shallow dishes. Carefully run a small, sharp knife around the edge of a soufflé cup, to loosen. Unmold the meringues and float in the sauce.

LEFT: Icons of New York City, real and in miniature. OPPOSITE: Humble sugar adds an instant wow factor when it's spun into an orb. Here on the twenty-two-mile-long island of Manhattan, we set ours atop *îles flottantes* (French for "floating islands" . . . get it?)—an isle of meringue atop thick, dreamy custard.

On the Road

A SIDECAR IN A SIDECAR

Ask any Manhattan messenger. The secret to getting around the city fast isn't the subway (*ha!*) or a car. It's having the ne plus ultra in freedom: *two-wheel drive*. I've biked around New York City for twenty years and built custom bikes for toting around everything from my farmer's market groceries to my kids. When people see me—often whirring around in a dress and heels, with my dog, Bobbin, in the sidecar—they can't help but laugh. Even served on terra firma, this sidecar recipe is a way to savor that feeling of being on my bike in the city, the wind in my hair.

ORANGE-KISSED SIDECAR
Makes 2

Ice cubes
½ cup brandy
¼ cup triple sec
¼ cup fresh orange juice
2 tablespoons fresh lemon juice

Fill a cocktail shaker with ice. Add the brandy, triple sec, and orange and lemon juices and shake vigorously. Strain into 2 coupe glasses, dividing evenly.

Farther Afield

In our often jam-packed days, America's grasslands are eternally alluring . . . in part because they're seemingly boundless, rolling in waves to the horizon line in every direction. Talk about free range! I can't help but take them as a party muse, from their patches of woods to their glass-clear lakes.

O f all the seasons worth celebrating on our annual calendar—from "holiday" to "football"—I've got another highly important one to add to the festivities: morel. When the trees are finally budding after the thaw in Jackson Hole, morel season has unofficially begun . . . and traipsing into the woods we go, with an experienced mushroom hunter, in search of these nutty, earthy treasures.

To celebrate morels in the fairy-tale manner they deserve, I arranged a woodland scene in a dense forest. A friend of my mom's made the felt tablecloth eons ago, and it couldn't have set a more folksy tone, with its charming owls and Seussian tree branches. Vintage plates I unearthed in Paris are painted with different outdoorsy satires, and even the buffet got into character—with slivers of tree stumps I cut myself (by chainsaw, no less). But one of my favorite elements were the teensy meringue mushrooms I served on branch slices under glass cloches. I couldn't find any small enough, so these cloches are actually lemon savers, of all things. The *morel* of the story? It's worth going the extra mile to make an already fun lunch an unforgettable one.

THESE PAGES: A handcrafted touch—such as this charming hand-stitched felt tablecloth—lends joy to any table. FOLLOWING PAGES: Vintage plates I found in Paris playfully depict picnic scenes.

Into the Woods

THE FRUITS OF THE STORYBOOK FOREST

ABOVE: Our beloved dog, Bobbin, patiently awaits a fallen morsel. OPPOSITE: Can you imagine this same table set with a standard ho-hum white cloth? Neither can I! FOLLOWING PAGES: Wood rounds exalt the alfresco buffet to new heights. I adore the tree sculpture, especially because it was hand-carved by my extremely talented nephew, Jack Rose.

CHAMPAGNE-CHAMOMILE COOLER WITH DRUNKEN RASPBERRIES

Makes 6 to 8 servings

DRUNKEN BERRIES
12 ounces fresh raspberries
1 cup best-quality raspberry preserves
½ cup Framboise (clear raspberry eau de vie)

PUNCH
4 cups brewed chamomile tea, well chilled
⅓ cup St-Germain elderflower liqueur
3 tablespoons freshly squeezed lemon juice
Ice mold* or 4 cups ice cubes
2 (750 ml) bottles Champagne or sparkling wine, well chilled

FOR THE BERRIES: Place the raspberries in a large, wide-mouthed jar. Using a potato masher or the back of a large spoon, roughly mash the berries. Mix in the jam and liqueur. (Can be prepared up to 1 day ahead. Seal the jar and refrigerate.)

FOR THE PUNCH: Stir the tea, St-Germain, and lemon juice in a punch bowl. Carefully add the ice mold or ice cubes. Pour in the Champagne. Serve the punch in glasses, allowing guests to sweeten individual servings with the desired amount of Drunken Berries.

*To make an ice mold: Select a tube pan, soufflé dish, or deep cake pan that measures about 3 inches smaller in diameter than your punch bowl. Fill the mold with water, leaving about 2 inches at the top. Add lemon slices, nonpoisonous leaves, and raspberries, arranging them in a decorative fashion (the ingredients will float). Freeze overnight or wrap the frozen mold tightly and freeze up to 1 month. To release, turn the mold upside down and place under running water until the ice releases.

THESE PAGES: Punching up our forested fun: a Champagne chamomile cooler with drunken raspberries (served in earthy ceramic cups, of course). Note to self: Raspberry jam makes an excellent sweetener for cocktails.

CLOCKWISE FROM TOP LEFT: Just-plucked honeycomb leaves guests abuzz. I love to use vintage ceramic vases rather than glass; they add so much texture and character! These place cards are from an Etsy seller and are a fun way to bring more details to the theme. OPPOSITE: A ceramic pie bird serves a very important function by venting piping-hot steam from below the crust into the autumn air.

WILD MUSHROOM AND FONTINA FLATBREAD
Makes one 12-inch flatbread

½ ounce dried morel mushrooms
Extra-virgin olive oil
5 ounces assorted mushrooms, such as shiitake, chanterelle,
    or oyster, sliced
1 garlic clove, minced
2 teaspoons fresh thyme leaves, minced
Kosher salt
All-purpose flour
8 ounces pizza dough
1½ cups (about 6 ounces) grated Italian fontina cheese
2 tablespoons freshly grated Parmesan

Rinse any dirt or grit from the dried morels. Soak the morels in a bowl of warm water until softened, 30 minutes to 1 hour. Drain well and cut into 1-inch pieces.

Heat 1 tablespoon olive oil in a large, heavy skillet over medium-high heat. Add the morels and sliced mushrooms and sauté until just tender, about 4 minutes. Add the garlic and thyme and sauté until the mushrooms are tender and dry, about 2 minutes. Season the mushrooms with salt. (Can be prepared up to 2 days ahead. Transfer to a small container and refrigerate.)

Position one rack in the top third and one rack in the bottom third of the oven and preheat to 400°F. Sprinkle a large, heavy sheet pan lightly with flour (about 1 tablespoon). Roll the dough out on a lightly floured surface to a 12-inch round. Transfer the round to the prepared sheet pan. Brush dough lightly with olive oil. Sprinkle the fontina cheese evenly over the dough. Distribute the mushrooms evenly over the cheese. Sprinkle the Parmesan over the mushrooms. Bake the flatbread on the bottom rack until the crust is golden brown on the bottom, about 15 minutes. Transfer the flatbread to the top rack and bake until the top is golden brown, about 3 minutes. Transfer the flatbread to a cutting board, cut into wedges, and serve.

THESE PAGES: **The only thing better than morels? Morel-topped "pizza," such as these wild mushroom and fontina flatbreads.**

THESE PAGES: Meringue mushroom caps become even more storybook when nestled under glass-dome cloches. (*Psst*: actually, they're lemon savers I found online.)

Petals & Palomas

A LUNCHEON IN FULL BLOOM

Flowers are proof that the universe loves us and wants us to be happy. After a winter of drudgery—gray skies, grayer moods—they burst forth in all their Technicolor glory and make everyone around them feel reborn, too. And to me, there are no flowers like the spring wildflowers in Texas. Who *wouldn't* want to soak up their fanciful splendor?

Last spring I hauled a tin-topped table and leather safari chairs out into the pasture with some of my nearest and dearest. Our mission: to don our prettiest dresses and treat ourselves to edible flower-topped fare while sipping Prettier Paloma cocktails (a beloved grapefruit tequila tipple, made throughout the Rio Grande region since the invention of citrusy Squirt soda in 1938).

In a setting so lush and luxuriant, I couldn't help but design a table to suit. Juxtaposed against the industrial tabletop, the plethora of blossoms felt extra bewitching. I don't believe you can ever have too many flowers, so I topped deviled eggs and buttery sugar cookies with edible flowers and even nestled cuttings of cupcake cosmos into the pink palomas themselves. Sometimes fairy tales do come true—for an afternoon, at least.

THESE PAGES: Steeping yourself in prettiness is a form of self-care that's absolutely required every once in a while. And what's more flouncy and fanciful than wildflowers? For this ladies' luncheon, we dragged our tin-topped table right into a field of them. *X* marks the spot.

PREVIOUS PAGES: Pink buckets salvaged from a Lela Rose fashion show make a basic pickup truck bed look camera-ready. THESE PAGES: Vintage vases stocked with blooms, place cards emblazoned with pressed flowers, and flower-topped deviled eggs are elegance incarnate.

PRETTIER PALOMA

Makes 1

¼ cup pink grapefruit juice

3 tablespoons silver tequila

1 tablespoon fresh lemon juice, lemon half reserved,
    preferably Meyer

Flaky sea salt

Crushed and cubed ice

Grapefruit soda for finishing, such as Fever-Tree

Stir the grapefruit juice, tequila, and lemon juice in a cocktail
shaker. Sprinkle a small plate with salt. Run the reserved lemon
half around the rim of a coupe glass to moisten. Press the glass
into the salt to coat the rim. Fill the glass with crushed ice.
Add a few cubes of ice to the shaker and shake well. Pour the
drink over the crushed ice and top with soda to taste.

OPPOSITE: When you're outside, let your flower
arrangements go wild. RIGHT: Just-squeezed Meyer
lemon juice is one secret to a truly stellar paloma.
These blush and bashful pink coupes would make any
cocktail taste better . . . especially over crushed ice.

OPPOSITE: This antique silver serving piece was designed for serving candies and jellies but looks dynamite with upright deviled eggs. THIS PAGE: A blue-and-white woven wildflower dress (and matching shoes) complements Texas's wide-open skies perfectly. With their floral adornment, should we rename these deviled eggs angel eggs?

BLOSSOM SHORTBREAD COOKIES
Makes 24 to 36 (2- to 3-inch) cookies

2 cups all-purpose flour
3 tablespoons yellow cornmeal
1 teaspoon salt
1 cup (2 sticks) unsalted butter, room temperature
¾ cup powdered sugar
2 teaspoons vanilla extract
1½ teaspoons freshly grated lemon or orange zest
Edible flowers, such as pansies, dianthus, violas, chamomile, marigolds, and cornflowers
2 egg whites
White sparkling sugar for sprinkling

Stir the flour, cornmeal, and salt to blend in a medium bowl. In a large bowl, beat the butter, sugar, vanilla, and zest with an electric mixer until very light and fluffy. Gradually mix in the flour mixture. Gather the dough into a ball and divide in half. Shape the dough halves into discs, wrap in plastic, and chill 1 hour. (Dough can be made up to 4 days ahead. Allow the dough to soften slightly to room temperature before continuing.)

Preheat the oven to 300°F. Line large sheet pans with parchment paper. Working in batches, roll out one dough disc between sheets of parchment paper to a ¼-inch-thick round. Remove the top piece of parchment. Using 2- to 3-inch round cookie cutters, press the cutters gently onto the surface of the dough, without cutting through, to form a guide for the flowers. Arrange flowers decoratively on the rounds. Carefully replace the top sheet of parchment paper, being careful not to displace the flowers. Using a rolling pin, gently roll over the paper, pressing the flowers into the dough. Remove the top piece of parchment paper and cut out the rounds. Use a small spatula to transfer the cookies to the prepared sheet pans, spacing apart evenly.

Whisk the egg whites until frothy in a small bowl. Lightly brush the cookies with the egg white. Sprinkle the cookies with the sparkling sugar and bake until golden, about 18 minutes. Transfer the cookies to a rack to cool. (Cookies can be made up to 5 days ahead. Store in an airtight container.)

Berry Refreshing

A TIPPLE TO GO

When Covid-19 descended, I found a semblance of sanity by grabbing my hat and treating myself to long, meandering strolls. I would take epic ten-mile hikes through our ranch in Texas just to see what I could see, and it was beyond fascinating. One of my best discoveries: patches of wild blackberry brambles that pop up here and there like edible fireworks. I've been wandering here all my life, and I had no idea they existed!

Of course, whenever I happen upon wild berries—like the huckleberries I pile into my basket in late summer in Jackson Hole, then freeze and pop into my drinks all year long—I usually act like a doe-eyed deer and eat them. If you come across wild berries you recognize as edible, seize upon the opportunity. Plucked at the height of their ripeness, they are pillowy and sweet and put all grocery store varieties to shame. That summer, I used them to create a restorative and fizzy Blackberry Brambler cocktail, adorned with a stirrer emblazoned with our ranch's brand. I served it with "hogs in a blanket" (pastry-dough-wrapped local sausages) dipped in a blackberry *mostarda*. Energy bars just don't compare.

I'm always dashing out to pick blackberries in Texas or huckleberries in Jackson Hole—and dressing the part is very important! Here, I'm wearing an oversized hat for sun protection (wink, wink) and a collar stay by famed Navajo silversmith Esther Wood.

BLACKBERRY BRAMBLER
Serves 4

½ cup fresh blackberries, plus more for garnish
2 sprigs fresh thyme, plus more for garnish
1 cup bourbon whiskey
½ cup blackberry liqueur, such as Giffard Crème de Mûre
¼ cup fresh lemon juice
Ice cubes
Club soda or lemon seltzer to finish

Muddle the blackberries and thyme sprigs in a large pitcher. Add the bourbon, blackberry liqueur, and lemon juice and stir to blend. Fill 4 glasses with ice and divide the drink among the glasses. Top with soda to taste. Garnish the drinks with blackberries and thyme, and serve.

Custom wooden drink stirrers I ordered online give our Blackberry Bramblers—served in vintage tumblers, from a pitcher I received as a gift long ago—extra panache. I happened to have perfectly matching purple napkins with red embroidery in my stash of linens.

HOGS IN BLANKETS WITH BLACKBERRY MOSTARDA

Hogs in blankets are my elevated pigs in blankets. I use smoked sausages in place of hot dogs and puff pastry instead of crescent roll dough. Dufour brand puff pastry is my favorite, and I use an egg wash to create a glossy finish. Once baked, cut the "hogs" into pieces to serve with the *mostarda*. To make the "blankets," follow the package instructions for thawing and cut the pastry sheet into six even rectangles, about 4½ inches by 5 inches. Roll out each rectangle until it is approximately 7 inches long. Wrap each smoked sausage in the pastry rectangle, pressing the edges to seal. Vent the top of the pastry with a few diagonal lines. Transfer the "hogs" to a parchment-lined sheet pan, brush with egg wash, and bake in a 375°F oven until golden brown, about 15 minutes.

BLACKBERRY *MOSTARDA*
Makes about 1½ cups

Mostarda is a fruit-and-mustard condiment traditionally served in Italy. I add fresh blackberries to mine to serve with my "hogs."

1 tablespoon olive oil	2 tablespoons Dijon mustard
1 medium red onion, chopped	2 tablespoons brown sugar
1 pear, peeled, cored and diced	1 tablespoon chopped fresh
1 (6-ounce) basket or container	Italian parsley
fresh blackberries,	Salt
plus more for garnish	Freshly ground black pepper
½ cup dry white wine	Italian parsley leaves for garnish
¼ cup whole-grain	
Dijon mustard	

Heat the oil in a medium, heavy saucepan set over medium. Add the onion and sauté until tender, about 8 minutes. Add the pear, blackberries, wine, mustards, and brown sugar and cook until thickened to a jam consistency, stirring occasionally, about 12 minutes. Remove from the heat and stir in the parsley. Season to taste with salt and pepper. Transfer to a bowl or jar. (Can be prepared up to 4 days ahead; cover and refrigerate.) When ready to serve, garnish with parsley.

Hogs in a blanket deserve so much more, do they not? These smoked sausages are wrapped in puff pastry and served with a blackberry-pear *mostarda*. Divine.

South by Southwest

A QUINTESSENTIAL CRAWFISH BOIL

If you don't yet have a bestie from Louisiana, get one. Stat. My good friend Elliot is from New Orleans, and he has come out to the ranch a few times to help me host ebullient crawfish boils. A seasonal, regional staple originating with the Cajuns and the Creoles in the 1700s, crawfish boils are arguably the most fun way to throw a party for a crowd.

We recently held a crawfish boil for friends and family on the ranch. It couldn't have been easier. We drained the aromatic medley straight from the pot where it'd been boiling and served it on a table covered with newspaper: potatoes, corn, oranges, garlic, and of course, oodles of crawfish, which had turned as red as Calabrian chilis. No plates, no utensils.

To drink, we served another NOLA staple: Pimm's Cups, with a "build your own" twist I called Pimm's on Parade. Guests could adorn theirs with whatever beckoned, including slivers of cucumber and fishing lures that would help them ID which was theirs as the evening got a little, err, muddled. The best part of hosting a crawfish boil? At the end of the night, you just roll up the newspaper and toss it. Momma didn't raise no fool.

THESE PAGES: A fringed skirt always arrives ready to party. (This one in particular—part of our newly launched Lela Rose Ranch Collection—seems to echo the Indian blanket wildflowers that adorn Texas roadsides.)

THIS PAGE: You can never have too many muck boots, but who said they have to be a dull and dreary hunter green? We brought plenty of loaner sizes to share, plus baskets of other musts (including throw blankets, if a chill should arise off the lake.) OPPOSITE: If you love the concept of "island time"—that is, relaxation to the max—give "canoe time" a try. FOLLOWING PAGES: The most spectacular cooler imaginable.

OPPOSITE: Keep your Pimm's and ginger ale on ice—the colder they are, the more refreshed you and your guests will feel. LEFT: Pimm's Cups have stood the test of time for good reason—the combination of cucumber, lemon, and mint is forever refreshing! For my Pimm's on Parade, I couldn't help but add a fishing lure to each glass so guests could keep track of their tipple.

PIMM'S ON PARADE – PERSONALIZED PIMM'S CUPS
Serves 6 to 8

Originally created by the owner of a London oyster bar in the 1840s, this light and refreshing cocktail is the perfect cooler on warm summer day.

8 (½-inch-thick) unpeeled cucumber rounds or spears, from 1 hothouse cucumber
1 large unpeeled orange, cut into rounds
1 large unpeeled lemon, cut into rounds
1 large unpeeled apple, cored and cut into wedges
16 fresh mint sprigs
2 cups Pimm's No. 1 Cup
½ cup fresh lemon juice
2½ cups chilled ginger ale or lemon-lime soda
1½ cups chilled sparkling water
Ice cubes

Combine the cucumbers, fruit, and half the mint sprigs in a large pitcher. Using a muddler or the handle of wooden spoon, press on the fruit and mint several times. Add the Pimm's and lemon juice. Refrigerate for 1 hour, then mix in the ginger ale and sparkling water.

Fill glasses with ice cubes, then add the chilled punch and its fruits. Garnish with the remaining mint sprigs.

LEFT: A cucumber slice makes an excellent drink stirrer.
OPPOSITE: A garnish of chamomile adds a dash of pretty.

RIGHT AND FOLLOWING PAGES: A crawfish boil is low-maintenance—(Look, Ma! No tablecloths!)—but it feels luxurious, thanks to the overflowing abundance of food and seemingly bottomless drinks.

BAYOU CRAWFISH BOIL
Makes about 12 servings

Fresh crawfish are alive and must be cooked the day they are delivered. Many vendors provide bags of spice mix to be used in the boil, or you can try the fresh blend that I use. You will need an 80-quart outdoor seafood boiler, which can be purchased or rented from a restaurant supply or party rental store. The boiler will include a pot with a lid and an inner basket, an elevated base with a propane burner, and a long paddle stirrer. Be sure to purchase your onions in a mesh bag.

SPICE BLEND
⅓ cup whole cloves
¼ cup whole allspice
3 tablespoons black peppercorns
3 tablespoons coriander seeds
1 cup cayenne pepper
½ cup garlic powder
½ cup paprika
¼ cup dried oregano
¼ cup dried thyme
3 tablespoons onion powder

BOIL
1 (3-pound) mesh bag of yellow onions, labels and tags removed
3 heads garlic, halved
15 gallons water
3 pounds kosher salt
6 lemons, halved
4 oranges, halved
10 bay leaves, fresh or dried
5 pounds large red potatoes
12 ears corn, shucked and halved
1 large (30- to 35-pound) bag fresh live crawfish, cleaned
2 (5-pound) bags ice

FOR THE SPICE BLEND: Using a spice grinder or mill, coarsely grind the cloves, allspice, peppercorns, and coriander. Transfer the spices to a medium bowl and stir in the remaining ingredients. (Spice blend can be made up to 3 days ahead. Store covered at cool room temperature.)

FOR THE BOIL: Halve the onions and return them to the mesh bag. Add the garlic to the bag with the onions and tie to seal. Arrange the inner basket in the boiler pot and ignite the burner. Add the bag to the boiler pot, along with the water, salt, lemons, oranges, and bay leaves and bring to a boil. Add the potatoes and corn and boil 10 minutes. Stir in the crawfish and the spice blend; cover and return to a boil. Boil 3 minutes to partially cook the crawfish. Turn off the heat, cover the pot, and let rest 15 minutes to finish cooking the crawfish and vegetables. Add the ice to the pot to stop the cooking. When the ice melts, remove the inner basket to drain the crawfish and vegetables. Remove the bag of onions and garlic and transfer the crawfish and vegetables to a table and serve immediately.

BLACK MUSTARD SEED AND CUMIN ONION RINGS

Serves 12 to 16

This is my riff on Yotam Ottolenghi's famous onion rings. I changed up the seasonings to pair well with the ranch and crawfish.

8 cups buttermilk
1 cup white wine vinegar
4 cups all-purpose flour
3 tablespoons black mustard seeds
1 tablespoon ground cumin
1 tablespoon salt, plus more for seasoning
2 teaspoons finely grated lemon zest
1 generous teaspoon freshly ground black pepper
1 scant teaspoon cayenne pepper
3 very large onions, cut into rounds and separated into rings
2 bunches scallions or other green onions
Oil for deep-frying

Line 3 or 4 large sheet pans with wax paper. Mix the buttermilk and vinegar in a large bowl. In another large bowl, whisk the flour, mustard seeds, cumin, 1 tablespoon salt, zest, and black and cayenne peppers until well blended.

Working in batches, dip the onion rings into the flour mixture, shaking off the excess. Then dip the rings into the buttermilk mixture, and then back into the flour mixture until evenly coated. Arrange the onion rings on the sheet pans. Continue with the remaining onion rings and green onions.

Heat the oil in a deep fryer or large, heavy pot until the oil is between 350°F and 375°F on a deep-frying thermometer. Line a work surface or additional sheet pans with newspaper or paper towels. Working in batches, fry the onion rings and green onions, turning once or twice, until golden brown, about 3 minutes. Using a slotted spoon, carefully transfer the onions to the paper to drain. Sprinkle with salt and serve as soon as you can.

The only thing better than alfresco onion rings? Black mustard seed and cumin onion rings made to perfectly complement a crawfish boil with their spices and just-grated lemon zest.

Fourth of July

A NEW TOAST TO OLD GLORY

We the people of the United States, in order to form a more perfect party, need to try a little harder. At least when it comes to celebrating our nation's birthday. Let's be honest: the Fourth of July can become slightly underwhelming. Last July in Jackson Hole we did a few things to declare our independence from all the Fourth of July cheesiness. We started by setting the scene and pulling out our fabrics that say "Americana" at a glance: checks; red, white, and blue coverlets; gingham. We even found Lady Liberty tea towels to use as napkins!

For a patriotic yet summery drink, tequila-watermelon-basil coolers served in miniature watermelons did the trick—especially when accompanied by perfectly cubed, glass-clear ice, mini watermelon drink stirrers, and slivers of lime. I stand firm in my belief that hot dogs are the perfect July 4th food . . . we just need to elevate them a bit. That day, we nestled our spiraled, very high-quality links into brioche buns, with bowls of cornichon and sundry mustards for toppings. After dark, we trotted out to the levee to croon "God Bless America," waving our sparklers in the air like shooting stars.

We got lucky when Betsy Ross designed the flag. Red, white, and blue are such a jolly, bold trio, and they lend themselves perfectly to a height-of-summer table.

RED, WHITE, AND BOOZE (WATERMELON-BASIL COOLER)
Serves 4

¾ cup silver tequila
¼ cup mezcal or reposado tequila
1 jalapeño, halved lengthwise and seeded
4 mini watermelons
⅓ cup fresh lime juice
⅓ cup homemade or purchased basil simple syrup
Ice cubes
Lime slices for garnish

Stir the tequila, mezcal, and jalapeño in a large pitcher. Steep the jalapeño in the tequila mixture until the tequila mixture is lightly spiced, about 1 to 2 hours.

Meanwhile, using a large, sharp knife, cut off the top quarter of the watermelons. Cut a small slice off the rind (not flesh) of the opposite end of the watermelons so they can stand upright. Scoop out the watermelon flesh into a large bowl; reserve the watermelon "cups," chilled if possible.

Working in batches, puree the watermelon in a blender. Strain the pureed watermelon through a sieve set over a large bowl.

Remove the jalapeño halves from the tequila mixture and discard. Stir 2 cups of the watermelon puree into the tequila mixture, along with the lime juice and simple syrup. Refrigerate just until cold, about 1 hour. Refrigerate any remaining watermelon puree in a container and reserve for another use.

Fill the "cups" with ice and ladle in the punch, dividing evenly. Garnish with lime slices and serve.

TOP LEFT: Yes, I'm gaga for gingham . . . especially in the Americana summer-calendar sandwich between Memorial Day and Labor Day. I apply it liberally on the Fourth of July, from my statement necklace to my napkins. RIGHT: These tequila-watermelon coolers served in (yep) miniature watermelons are so fantastic, George Washington himself would have asked for seconds. (We simply sliced a small snip off the bottom of each one, so they'd sit flat on the picnic table.)

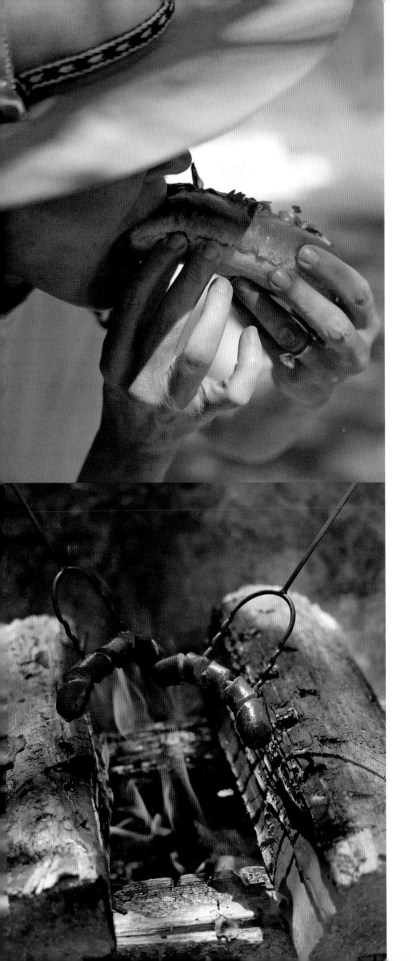

HAUTE DOGS WITH FANCY FIXINS
Makes 6 to 12 servings

12 best-quality hot dogs
12 brioche hot dog buns
Chopped, sautéed yellow onions
Chopped Italian parsley leaves
Cornichons (gherkins)
Mustard

To spiral-cut the hot dogs, place a hot dog on a cutting board. Using a small, sharp knife, cut into the hot dog at a slight angle. Turn the hot dog and continue cutting, being careful not to cut through the hot dog, until you reach the other end, creating a spiral. Repeat with the remaining hot dogs. Grill or skewer the hot dogs and cook over an open flame until they are browned and they sizzle. Serve the hot dogs with the buns, cheese sauce, onions, parsley, cornichons, and mustard.

Everybody loves a hot dog, but let's be honest: they're not a very extravagant dish. I like to upgrade mine just a touch by giving them a spiral cut before grilling and serving them atop brioche buns with toppings like cornichons. Haute dogs, indeed.

Mountain Majesty

Craggy, snow-dusted peaks. Crystalline streams. Elk, bighorn sheep, and moose aplenty as neighbors. Is it any wonder I love hosting events in the wilderness surrounding Jackson Hole, Wyoming? The cell service isn't always perfect...but the human connections we make here are.

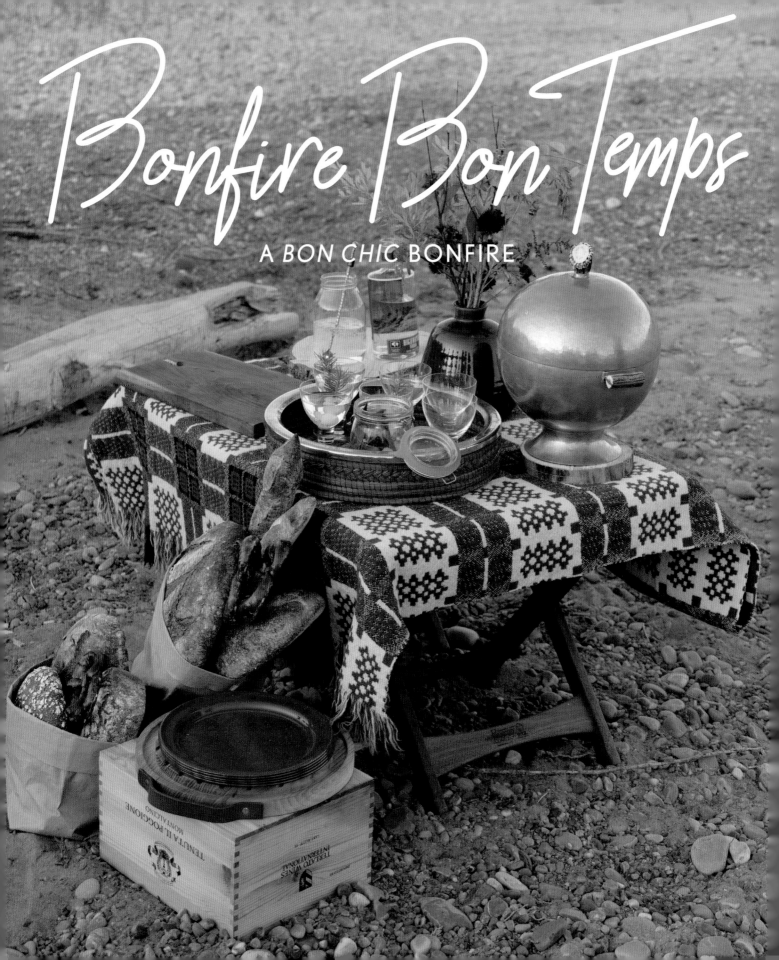

Bonfire Bon Temps

A BON CHIC BONFIRE

Our property in Jackson Hole backs up onto the Snake, one of the most pristine rivers in the nation and a go-to spot for bird-watching, fly-fishing, and . . . you guessed it! . . . hosting a party. In autumn, the water has receded so much that you can just stroll across it to little pop-up islands without anyone floating away.

Last year, we built a driftwood bonfire for the ages out there, with no threat of forest fire thanks to its perch between two flowing channels of water. It's downright magical being able to sit out there and listen to the Snake babble on by as the moon comes up and golden eagles fly overhead.

Because it's hard to do a full dinner such a schlep away from our kitchen, we opted for a simple menu of Gibson martinis with tipsy pearl onions and grilled oysters (shucked on-site!) with fabulous bread toasted over the fire, both served with *beurre vert* herbed butter. I enlisted my friends to help me tote everything over the water—the folding table, the enamelware. For a tablecloth? An antique Welsh Caernarvon blanket, a centuries-old textile that's so graphic it's forever modern—and can double as my wrap skirt and throw pillows. How Scarlett O'Hara!

THESE PAGES: A rocky atoll in the middle of the Snake River is a prime launchpad for a serious bonfire. (This one has a de facto tepee built around it for wind protection.) PREVIOUS PAGES: Nobody said bonfires have to be low-style. It was well worth it to tote out this 1960s pewter globe-shaped Hermès ice bucket with antler-horn handle on top for the evening . . . it's undoubtedly what Bond, James Bond, would do.

THIS PAGE: My obsession with antique Welsh Caernarvon blankets means I'm forever finding ways to use them—to fashion skirts, fringed throw pillows, even tablecloths. OPPOSITE: When I'm shopping for freshly baked breads from my artisanal bakery, I often try to get a variety of textures and flavors so carbaholics of every sort are satisfied.

GIBSON MARTINI WITH TIPSY PEARL ONIONS
Makes 1

⅓ cup gin
1 tablespoon dry vermouth
2-3 Tipsy Onions (see recipe)
Pine or rosemary spears

Combine the gin and vermouth in an ice-filled cocktail glass. Stir gently to chill. Strain the cocktail into a martini glass. Thread the onions onto a pine spear for the cocktail garnish.

TIPSY ONIONS
Makes about 2 cups

2 (8-ounce) or 1 (16-ounce) jar cocktail onions, drained
6 bay leaves (preferably fresh)
Large strips of lemon zest from 1 lemon
6 juniper berries
3 whole cloves
About 2 cups dry vermouth, divided

Drain the onions and transfer to a large, wide-mouthed heatproof jar. Place the bay leaves, lemon zest, juniper berries, and cloves in a small, heavy saucepan and stir to combine. Add ½ cup of the vermouth and bring the mixture to a simmer over medium heat. Pour the hot vermouth mixture over the onions in the jar. Add additional vermouth to cover. Seal the jar and refrigerate at least overnight and up to 1 month.

THESE PAGES: Call me a Gibson girl. These gin and dry vermouth cocktails—beloved since they were invented circa 1908—are garnished with "tipsy onions" steeped in vermouth and juniper berries . . . and put a standard martini to shame.

BEURRE VERT
Makes about 2 cups

Grill oysters with mini knobs of this flavorful emerald-hued butter, then thickly spread any remaining butter on campfire-toasted bread to serve with the Herbed Onion Bouillon.

2 bunches trimmed fresh chives, cut into 1-inch pieces
½ cup packed fresh parsley leaves
1 small shallot, sliced
1½ cups (3 sticks) unsalted butter, at room temperature
2 teaspoons finely grated lemon zest
1 teaspoon fine sea salt
1 teaspoon freshly ground black pepper

Line a small cake pan or bowl with plastic wrap. Process the chives, parsley, and shallot in a food processor until finely chopped. Add the butter, lemon zest, salt, and pepper and process until the butter and herbs are well blended. Season to taste with additional salt and pepper. Transfer the butter to the prepared pan, smoothing the top. Cover and chill until firm. (Can be prepared up to 1 week ahead.)

THESE PAGES: The world becomes even more of your oyster when you top your bivalves with a gorgeous compound butter of chive, shallot, lemon, and black pepper.

HERBED ONION BOUILLON

Makes about 6 servings

Use homemade or your favorite purchased bone broth for this rustic, warming soup. High-quality bone broth can be found in the freezer section of your grocery store or at your local butcher.

2 tablespoons butter
2 yellow onions, cut into ½-inch-thick slices
¼ cup dry white wine
8 cups beef bone broth
2 bay leaves, preferably fresh
2 sprigs fresh thyme
1 sprig fresh rosemary
Kosher salt
Freshly ground black pepper

Melt the butter in a heavy pot over medium heat. Add the onions and sauté until golden brown, about 12 minutes. Add the wine and simmer until the liquid evaporates, about 3 minutes. Pour in the broth and add the bay leaves, thyme, and rosemary. Cover and simmer over low heat to allow the flavors to meld, about 30 minutes. Season to taste with salt and pepper. (Can be prepared up to 4 days ahead, covered and refrigerated. Return broth to a simmer before serving.)

THESE PAGES: In the last few years, bone broth has become on-trend for a very good reason: not only is it immune-and collagen-boosting (hallelujah!), but it's also undeniably delicious. There's no better soup than this Herbed Onion Bouillon after the sun goes down. Serve with the crustiest artisanal loaves of bread you can find topped with the *beurre vert*, and it's unforgettable.

A Patchwork Picnic

DELIGHT, STITCH BY STITCH

love (*loooove*) old quilts. Their geometry, their colors, the fact that they're things of beauty often patchworked together from hand-me-down fabrics. It's no wonder they often become heirlooms, passed down from one generation of cuddlers to the next. I have hoarded tons of them over the years, the more vintage-y and timeworn the better. So when I discovered the work of ceramist Lydia Johnson, who transforms thin slab-built ceramics into colorful, folk-quilt-effect tableware that reads as light and airy as fuzzy dandelion seeds, I just about fell out of my chair. I commissioned her to make mugs and plates, and the collection spurred the coziest Jackson Hole lakeside picnic for my girlfriends.

In such an Americana setting, serving nostalgic foods seemed like a must. Our menu that afternoon? Fried green tomato and country ham biscuits, lemon tarts, and spirited lavender iced tea. As the sun streamed down and a bald eagle circled overhead, I felt like we were reenacting an old-fashioned quilt circle full of laughter in stitches—just swap in free-flowing drinks for the actual needlework.

OPPOSITE AND FOLLOWING PAGES: I don't like to make blanket statements, but...how perfect are quilts? Colorful, happy, and nostalgic—they make comfy party backdrops for a picnic by the pond with girlfriends.

PREVIOUS PAGES, ABOVE, AND RIGHT: Quilt-inspired tableware by ceramist Lydia Johnson has all the graphic appeal of timeworn quilts, especially juxtaposed alongside plum-colored stemware. OPPOSITE: This particular quilt is a hexagonal pattern, as riveting as honeycomb.

SPIRITED LAVENDER ICED TEA

Makes about 12 servings

Butterfly pea flowers from Thailand are what give this cooler its lovely lavender hue—look for them at specialty tea shops, health food stores, or online.

3 bags green tea
2½ tablespoons dried butterfly pea flowers
1 tablespoon dried culinary lavender
1 cup sugar
2 cups vodka
¾ cup fresh lemon juice, about 2 lemons
Ice cubes
Lavender honey
Merlot salt
Fresh lavender flower sprigs

Bring 8 cups water to a boil in a large saucepan. Remove from the heat and immediately add the green tea, pea flowers, and lavender. Cover and steep until cool. Strain the tea through a fine-mesh sieve into a pitcher or beverage dispenser. Mix in the sugar; stir to dissolve. Stir in the vodka and lemon juice. Refriger-ate until cold, at least 2 hours and up to 8 hours. Remove the pitcher from the refrigerator and add ice.

TO SERVE: Using a small pastry brush, paint a stripe of honey on one side of a glass and sprinkle the honey with the salt to coat. Add ice to the glass and fill with the cooler. Garnish with a lavender flower.

PREVIOUS PAGES AND THESE PAGES: **The only thing more relaxing than an afternoon of giggles by the pond is enjoying it with a spirited lavender iced tea. Lavender has curative properties, but I find it boosts my feelings of wellness even more with a dash of vodka!**

FRIED GREEN TOMATO, HAM, AND CHEDDAR BISCUIT SANDWICHES

Makes about 16 sandwiches

BLACK PEPPER CORNMEAL BISCUITS
1¾ cups all-purpose flour, plus more for dusting
¼ cup yellow cornmeal
1 tablespoon baking powder
1 scant teaspoon coarsely ground black pepper
¼ teaspoon fine sea salt
4 tablespoons (½ stick) unsalted butter, chilled and
   cut into small pieces, plus 2 tablespoons melted
¾ cup buttermilk

TOMATOES
1½ cups all-purpose flour
1 teaspoon fine sea salt, plus more for sprinkling
½ teaspoon freshly ground black pepper
2 cups yellow cornmeal
1 cup plain dry bread crumbs

4 large eggs
½ cup buttermilk
1 pound medium green tomatoes, cut into ¼-inch-thick slices
Vegetable oil, for frying

BISCUIT SANDWICHES
Mayonnaise
About 8 ounces thinly sliced or shaved ham
About 8 ounces white cheddar cheese, sliced
Fresh dill sprigs

FOR THE BISCUITS: Preheat the oven to 450°F. Line a large sheet pan with parchment paper.

Mix the flour, cornmeal, baking powder, pepper, and salt in a large bowl. Using a pastry blender, blend the chilled butter into the flour until it resembles coarse meal. Using a fork, stir in the buttermilk. Gather the dough and turn out onto a lightly floured board.

Using floured hands, flatten the dough to a thickness of ½ inch. Cut the dough with a floured 2-inch biscuit cutter, rerolling scraps as necessary to make 16 biscuits. Space the biscuits evenly on the prepared pan. Brush the biscuits with the melted butter. Bake until lightly browned, 10 to 12 minutes. Transfer to a rack to cool completely.

FOR THE TOMATOES: Combine the flour, salt, and pepper on a plate. Blend the cornmeal and bread crumbs on another plate. Whisk the eggs and buttermilk in a medium bowl. Line a sheet pan with wax paper. Working in batches, dip the tomato slices into the flour mixture to lightly coat. Then dip into the buttermilk mixture, and finally into the cornmeal mixture. Transfer the breaded tomatoes to the prepared pan.

Line a plate with paper towels. Heat 1 inch oil in a large, heavy skillet until hot but not smoking. Fry the tomatoes until golden on each side, about 4 minutes per side. Transfer to the plate to drain.

FOR THE BISCUIT SANDWICHES: Split the biscuits in half and spread with mayonnaise. Top the bottom halves with ham and cheese slices, then tomato and dill. Add the biscuit tops and serve.

Let the River Run

A FLY-FISHING FETE

This late-summer dinner party was inspired by its location: the Snake River levee behind our property in Jackson Hole. I brought along rods and reels to loan to any friends who didn't have them for the afternoon's activity: fly-fishing for cutthroat and rainbow trout in the glass-clear waters below. Rainbow trout deserve their name. Their glitzy scales often range in ombré hues from salmon pink and lilac to aspen-leaf green and soft earth browns. What gorgeous colors for a tablescape! I borrowed each and every one for this event, knowing they'd look incredible rendered in napkins and tableware against the adjacent backdrop. (Pro tip: Colors cribbed from nature always "go" together.)

Guests nibbled smoked trout pâté and popovers and sipped Whiskey River cocktails named after the Willie Nelson song. It was the centerpiece, though, that really made them swoon. Instead of just using expected flowers in the middle of the table, I settled fallen branches covered in thick chartreuse moss my sister-in-law and I came upon while hiking. Adding something like that to your tabletop—something you could never buy, not for all the money in the world—makes it come alive.

OPPOSITE: So much thought and style seem to go into each and every fly-fishing fly that it's a shame to limit them to the task at hand. A few of mine became a conversation-starting showpiece of a vest, perfect for this trout-inspired dinner!

LEFT: The shimmering, showstopping beauty of cutthroat and rainbow trout kicked off the organic beauty of this dinner table in mints, browns, lilacs, and salmons. We used flower frogs to tuck stems of dahlias and other blooms between the mossy branches. BELOW: My mom found these vintage plates at a garage sale, and talk about luck: they're from famed Texas chef Helen Corbitt (a leading chef of the Neiman Marcus Zodiac Room). OPPOSITE: Hurricane taper holders keep the candles lit even after a breeze picks up.

WHISKEY RIVER
Makes 1

Ice cubes
⅓ cup Wyoming Whiskey or Bourbon
2 tablespoons fresh orange juice
2 tablespoons fresh lemon juice
1 tablespoon maple syrup
Orange slice and mint sprig for garnish

Fill a shaker and glass with ice. Combine the whiskey, orange juice, lemon juice, and maple syrup in the shaker and shake to blend. Strain the cocktail into the glass and garnish with an orange slice and mint sprig.

LEFT: A chummy fly-fishing bear presides over the bar, standing tall on a cheeky book, *The Cocktail Hour in Jackson Hole*. OPPOSITE: Our Whiskey River cocktails are a perfect pairing with smoked trout pâté.

SMOKED TROUT PÂTÉ WITH POPOVERS

Makes 12 servings

Serve the pâté with homemade or purchased popovers.

16 ounces smoked trout fillets (about 2), skin and bones removed
1⅓ cups whole milk cottage cheese
¼ cup crème fraîche
½ cup snipped fresh chives
½ cup chopped fresh tarragon leaves
2 teaspoons grated lemon zest
Salt
Freshly ground black pepper

Crumble the trout into a bowl. Add the cottage cheese, crème fraîche, half of the chives, and all of the tarragon and lemon zest. Stir with a wooden spoon until very well blended. Season to taste with salt and pepper. (Can be prepared up to 2 days ahead, covered and refrigerated.) Garnish with the remaining chives before serving.

THESE PAGES: Crackers, schmackers. Eggy, fluffy popovers are ideal with our smoked trout pâté, made with crème fraîche and freshly plucked chives and tarragon.

Fire in the Hole

LUXE CAMPFIRE CANAPÉS

Truth? I am not the girl that's going to go camping and eat freeze-dried rice and beans. I have no interest in that *at all*. I do a ton of outdoorsy stuff, but I take my provisions seriously. I wrap my sandwiches in those adorable checked deli papers (Ziploc is a four letter word!), and serve manchego (a hard cheese that maintains its body) with some fabulous quince jam alongside. For me, part of the pleasure of being out in the wilderness is having fabulous food, so I'm always in search of inspiring—yet lightweight and packable—meals.

When my husband, son, and I recently climbed the Grand Teton—the highest peak in the entire range, at 13,775 feet—we carried with us these little bison pies decorated with camping scenes that I devised and baked ahead of time. We didn't actually make it to the summit that day, but when you wake up at 3:30 a.m. and are able to devour these in your rustic mountain hut as other hikers attempt to enjoy their packets of oatmeal . . . well, I felt like I had a grand achievement on the day of our Grand failure.

I love making food adorable. Whether I'm backpacking or just headed out for a creekside picnic, gorgeousness ranks alongside deliciousness and portability!

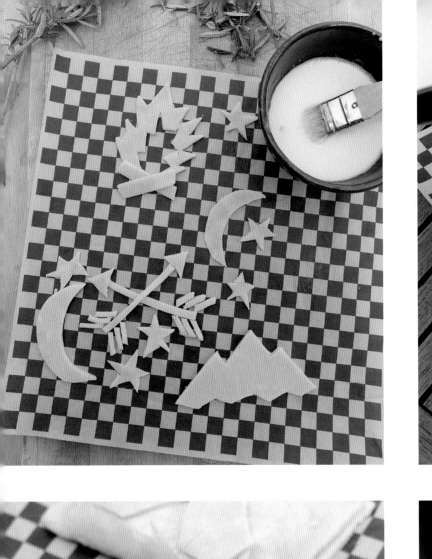

BESPOKE BISON HAND PIES

Makes 6

CRUST

3⅓ cups all-purpose flour, plus more for dusting

1 scant teaspoon salt

1 large egg

3 or 4 tablespoons sour cream

1 cup plus 2 tablespoons (2¼ sticks) unsalted butter, chilled and cut into small pieces

FILLING

1 tablespoon olive oil

1 large sweet onion, chopped

1 large Granny Smith apple, peeled, cored, and diced

2 tablespoons butter

1 pound ground bison

2 garlic cloves, minced

¼ cup white wine

2 tablespoons minced fresh Italian parsley leaves

2 teaspoons minced fresh rosemary

1 scant teaspoon salt

Freshly ground black pepper

1 egg

2 tablespoons milk

FOR THE CRUST: Stir the flour and salt to blend in a large bowl. Whisk the egg and 3 tablespoons sour cream to blend in a small bowl. Using a pastry blender, blend the butter into the flour mixture until it resembles coarse meal. Using a fork, stir the egg mixture into the flour mixture, adding the remaining sour cream if the dough appears dry. Gather the dough into two balls, and flatten into discs. Wrap the dough in wax paper and chill for 2 hours or up to 4 days.

THESE AND FOLLOWING PAGES: **One hidden thrill of pie crust is knowing that—thanks to the sturdiness of butter, eggs, and flour—it can do wondrous, artful things. When we're trekking into the woods, I love to decorate hand pies with very on-theme motifs, like campfires, pup tents, and starry skies.**

FOR THE FILLING: Heat the oil in a large, heavy skillet on medium-high. Add the onion and the apple and sauté until tender, about 10 minutes. Add the butter, then the bison and garlic to the pan, and cook, breaking up the meat with a wooden spoon, until browned, about 8 minutes. Add the wine, parsley, and rosemary and cook just until the liquid evaporates, about 1 minute. Season with the salt and pepper. Transfer to a bowl and cool completely. (Filling can be made up to 3 days ahead, covered, and refrigerated.)

Preheat the oven to 400°F. Line a large sheet pan with parchment. Whisk the egg and milk in a small bowl. Roll out each piece of pie dough on a lightly floured surface to an approximately 15-by-8-inch rectangle, trimming to form straight edges. Cut each rectangle into thirds, creating six 5-by-8-inch rectangles. Gather and reroll the scraps. Cut decorations from the scraps, if desired. Spoon ⅙ of the filling (about ½ cup) onto the short end of a rectangle. Brush the egg wash around the filling, then fold the rectangle in half, enclosing the filling completely. Gently press the edges to seal, then crimp with a fork. Transfer the pies to the prepared pan and repeat with the remaining filling and dough. Lightly brush the tops of the pies with the egg wash and add dough decorations, if using. Brush the decorations with the egg wash and bake until the crust is golden brown, about 20 minutes. Transfer to a platter and serve.

EL DIABLO EN FUEGO
Makes 1

The drink is great without the pyrotechnics, but if you do want a fire show, make a trip to a well-stocked liquor store to pick up 100-proof (or more) tequila.

⅓ cup reposado tequila
2 tablespoons crème de cassis
2 tablespoons fresh lime juice
½ lime, pulp removed and discarded
Sugar cube
1 tablespoon 100-proof tequila
⅓ cup ginger beer

Combine the reposado tequila, crème de cassis, and lime juice in a shaker. Set aside. Put the lime half on a plate and set the sugar cube in the center of the lime. Pour the high-proof tequila on top of the sugar cube. Fill a mug to the top with ice, give the shaker a shake, and add the contents to the mug. Top with the ginger beer. Carefully set the lime half atop the ice. Set the sugar cube aflame with a match or lighter. Serve immediately.

OPPOSITE: I always think it's important to make things fun—especially when you're pushing yourself out of your indoorsy comfort zone to get into the wilderness. And what's more fun than a flaming cocktail?

A Trail-Mix Tailgate

PULL UP A CHAIR

For certain bridal showers, hosting the same old luncheon won't do—especially when you long to spend time together outdoors, getting into nature and doing something different. I always love a group hike in the Wyoming wildlands, where we'd have deer, not dress, sightings and trail mix in lieu of tea. So I recently made an old Ford Bronco our party base camp and saddled up a make-your-own-trail-mix bar alongside it, with little paper sacks of cashews, chocolate chips, dried bananas, pepitas, raisins, and more.

After trekking through wildflower-strewn meadows and under lodgepole pines in the Gros Ventre Wilderness, we came back to a secret lunch hideaway to picnic on sandwiches and fancy-pants ants on a log reborn anew with chèvre and a rainbow's worth of sliced vegetables. The custom napkins doubled as bandanas everyone could wear around their necks like an old cowhand. We drank antioxidant-rich beet cocktails from enamelware mugs emblazoned with a Grand Teton National Park motif and hung from a bar fashioned out of sticks I found on a hike (sometimes adorableness doesn't cost a thing, folks).

LEFT: The origins of trail mix are murky, but my favorite tale dates to 1960s California—when surfers mingled nuts with dried fruit to power up for their day on the waves. There's nothing better to get you ready for outdoor adventure, especially when you can mix your own.

BEET ROSE COCKTAIL

Makes 10

1 (750 ml) bottle lemon-flavored vodka
2½ cups purchased fresh beet juice
1 cup lemon juice
Honey or simple syrup, to taste
Ice cubes
Mint sprigs for garnish
1 to 2 (750 ml) bottles Prosecco

Stir the vodka, beet juice, and lemon juice to combine in a large beverage dispenser. Add ice to fill and a few mint sprigs.

TO SERVE: Fill glasses with ice. Add enough of the vodka mixture to fill the glass halfway. Pour in enough Prosecco to fill the glass to the top. Garnish with mint sprigs.

THESE PAGES: Tucked in the shade and stocked with ice, your cocktail dispenser should stay cool until you return from your hike. I served these fizzy beet rose cocktails in Grand Teton National Park mugs and glasses wrapped in rattan that are easy to hold on to.

THESE PAGES: Everything I brought for our lunch that afternoon was grab and go, with no trash (aside from the parchment paper sandwich wrapping that we could tote out in our pockets). And who wants a paper napkin when a Grand Teton National Park cotton version can do double duty as a kerchief? Leave no trace . . . not even a tipple!

Ants on a log doesn't have to be kindergarten fare. Why not fancy-pants these ants with goat cheese, pine nuts, freshly snipped herbs, and a rainbow of rondelle-sliced vegetables (the brighter, the better)?

ROASTED RED BEET HUMMUS
Makes about 2 cups

Serve the hummus with assorted baby vegetables and chips.

1 (16-ounce) can chickpeas, drained and rinsed
2 medium roasted red beets, peeled and cut into pieces
²⁄₃ cup tahini
1 tablespoon lemon zest
¹⁄₃ cup fresh lemon juice, plus more if needed
2 garlic cloves
1 teaspoon cumin
1 teaspoon salt
¹⁄₃ cup extra-virgin olive oil, plus more for serving
Thinly sliced radish
Toasted pine nuts
Chopped fresh Italian parsley

Combine the chickpeas, beets, tahini, lemon zest and juice, garlic, cumin, and salt in a food processor and pulse several times until finely chopped. With the motor running, slowly add the olive oil and blend until smooth. Season to taste with additional salt and lemon juice, if necessary. (Can be prepared up to 4 days ahead, covered, and refrigerated.)

Transfer the hummus to a shallow bowl and drizzle with olive oil. Garnish with radish slices, pine nuts, and parsley.

LEFT: Butterflies can't help but land on such a sweet scene. An earthy wooden bowl is a fitting perch for vegetable chips. OPPOSITE: One of many things that makes my heart skip a *beet*? Rouge-pink hummus, thanks to a couple of roasted beets in the recipe. Adorn your bowl with pine nuts, sliced radishes, and a dusting of chopped parsley to elicit extra oohs and aahs.

Sundowner

TAKING TWILIGHT IN STYLE

had never heard of the concept of a "sundowner"— where you pull up to an abundant spread of cocktails and snacks in a jaw-dropping spot—until I went on my first safari in the Serengeti. It was so fabulous that I vowed then and there to bring the concept home to Wyoming, where the scenery and wildlife are, frankly, just as majestic (and the sunsets themselves every bit as glorious).

Hosting a sundowner makes my job as the host easy, because all I have to do is provide the food and drink . . . Mother Nature supplies the rest of the ambience. Sunsets have transfixed everyone from Claude Monet (who painted them again and again, determined to capture their mystical light) to Neil Young (who crooned about the land of beauty, space, and light in his song "California Sunset"). Don't they deserve a toast? So early last autumn, we toted leather camp chairs, armfuls of freshly cut sunflowers, and addictive nibbles and drinks into the fields below the 13,775-foot-high Tetons, including sweet potato chips with caviar and crème fraîche, and Turmeric Gin and Ginger Mules that glowed like the setting sun. It was so simple—just sitting out there together, watching the sun go down—and yet it couldn't have been more magical.

THESE PAGES: Given our sundowner theme, I chose sunflowers— which follow the sun from dawn until dusk—as a fitting inspiration. The flowers are indigenous to North America and have been growing boldly since circa 3000 BCE.

HOMEMADE SWEET POTATO CHIPS WITH CAVIAR AND CRÈME FRAÎCHE

Makes about 6 cups

The mild sweetness of these potato chips balances perfectly with rich crème fraîche and salt-and-sea-kissed caviar.

2 long (2-inch-diameter) sweet potatoes
Vegetable oil for frying
Flaky sea salt

Fill a large bowl with water. Peel and thinly slice the sweet potatoes into rounds. Place the sweet potatoes in the water and let stand 1 hour.

When ready to fry, drain the sweet potatoes and pat them dry between clean dish towels. Heat the oil to 365°F in a deep fryer or large, heavy saucepan. Line 2 large sheet pans with paper towels. Working in batches, fry the sweet potatoes until golden brown and crisp, about 3 minutes. Transfer to the paper towels to drain. Sprinkle with flaky sea salt.

LEFT: At sundown, a chill can settle over the land in Jackson Hole fairly quickly (it is at 6,237 feet in elevation, after all). Cozy sweaters are vital. OPPOSITE: Just as important: comfort foods. For nibbling we served housemade sweet potato chips, caviar with crème fraîche, and perfectly roasted almonds.

TURMERIC GIN AND GINGER MULE
Makes 2

Ice cubes
⅓ cup lemon gin (such as Sipsmith)
½ teaspoon ground turmeric
2 tablespoons fresh lemon juice
About 8 ounces ginger beer, chilled
2 lemon wedges for garnish

Fill 2 glasses and a cocktail shaker with ice. Add the gin, turmeric, and lemon juice to the shaker and shake vigorously. Pour over the ice and top with ginger beer. Garnish with a lemon wedge.

THESE PAGES: There's something instantly warming about a spicy turmeric cocktail—even one served with a squeeze of lemon on a craggy mountain of chipped ice.

RECIPE INDEX

ACKNOWLEDGMENTS

Sure, I can have fun solo (that's me "gone fishin'" with my Norwich terrier, Bobbin). But it takes a village to have a party, and creating a book like this is no different. It couldn't have happened without the assistance and mental magic of:

Jill Cohen and Melissa Powell, book packagers and problem solvers extraordinaire.

Kathryn O'Shea-Evans, my writer, Kathleen Jayes, my editor, and Rizzoli's publisher, Charles Miers, who believed in my vision from the start.

Jeanne Kelly, who whipped up many of these recipes and styled the food so these pages look good enough to eat.

Tara Sgroi, who photographed each soiree. Thank you for your fabulous eye and cheery disposition!

Doug Turshen and Steve Turner, designers who gave the layouts their fresh air.

Andrew Bourke and Jess Maupin—a true mountain man and his forever filly. From fording rivers, building bonfires, and calling in cows to modeling in between, this duo was there for it all.

Sam Masters, who corralled all my ideas for this book and helped turn them into shooting stars.

My fantastic staff—then and now—at Lela Rose: Adriene, Alia, Arianna, Ashlynne, Audye, Betsy, Casey, Chloe, Chong, Christina, Courtney, Crystal, Demi, Dimitra, Elise, Elizabeth, Erin, Francie, Hadassah, Haley, Hallie, Hanna, Iva, Jay, Jessica, Judy, Karen, Kevin, Leonora, Linda, Maggie, Mei, Piper, Roma, Sadie, Sarah, Su Ha, Susannah, Vinecia, Wendy, Yumiko, and Zachary. Even Mondays are a party with you all at the office.

My father, Rusty Rose, who connected me so much to the outdoors through his love of birds and sitting in nature, enjoying its serenity. You will live on forever in the lives you touched and through every hawk and meadowlark that soars above our ranch.

My mother, Deedie Rose. She taught me how to cook, sew, and altogether enjoy life and parties. She loved to entertain! She also gave me a priceless heirloom: my unending quest for learning and zest for life.

Catherine Rose, my sister-in-law and partner in crime. You're the most creative wordsmith I know and always willing to scurry up a hiking trail to scrounge for centerpiece decor, and I'm forever grateful.

Rick and Angy Bruce, and the Bruce family, who care for Rey Rosa and have kept it the ranch of my dad's dreams.

My husband, Brandon Jones. You put up with me and my crazy entertaining—and you're a Michelin-worthy sous chef to boot. You've always supported me in life, business, and family, and you're the best compadre a girl could have.

My kids, Grey and Rosey Jones. You are constant entertainment, and my life would not be complete without you. What a joy it is to be your mother!!

Finally, a thank you to my muses: the fields, mountains, and skies above. You're the ultimate excuse for a party.

RESOURCES

Creative Candles, creativecandles.com

Disco Cubes, discocubes.com

Ebay, ebay.com

Estelle Colored Glass, estellecoloredglass.com

Etsy, etsy.com

JonNiPaperGoods, etsy.com/shop/JonNiPaperGoods

Juliska, juliska.com

Lela Rose Ranch Collection, lelarose.com

Lydia Johnson Ceramics, lydiajohnsonceramics.com

Mason, Texas bootmaker, no website.
Look for his shop in downtown Mason, Texas, across from the courthouse. He is there most days from 9 a.m. to 5 p.m.

Ted Muehling, tedmuehling.com

Texas Quail Farms, texquail.com

First published in the United States of America in 2023 by
Rizzoli International Publications, Inc.
300 Park Avenue South
New York, NY 10010
www.rizzoliusa.com

Copyright © 2023 Lela Rose
Text: Kathryn O'Shea Evans

All images by Tara Sgroi except:
Lisa Flood: page 12, 226-227, 255, reverse of back endpapers
Carrie Patterson: pages 52, left 53, 230-241
Taylor Jewel: pages 92-99, bottom left 253
Ryan Goodrich: pages 148-153, 166, 168, 170, 171

Floral design by: Leah Meltzer of Serracina and Gina Humphries of Gina Humphries Floral Design

Publisher: Charles Miers
Senior Editor: Kathleen Jayes
Design: Doug Turshen with Steve Turner
Production Manager: Barbara Sadick
Managing Editor: Lynn Scrabis

Developed in collaboration with Jill Cohen Associates, LLC

Printed in China

2023 2024 2025 2026 / 10 9 8 7 6 5 4 3 2 1

ISBN: 978-0-8478-7295-4

Library of Congress Control Number: 2022945710

Visit us online:
Facebook.com/RizzoliNewYork
Twitter: @Rizzoli_Books
Instagram.com/RizzoliBooks
Pinterest.com/RizzoliBooks
Youtube.com/user/RizzoliNY
Issuu.com/Rizzoli